"Mark and Takara have discovered a simple and innovative approach to understanding and practically applying the Law of Attraction in your life. Their science-based system behind 'The Secret' is the 'how to' guide that will help you experience more success and accelerate your journey from where you are to where you want to be."

- **Jack Canfield**, co-author of the #1 New York Times best-selling *Chicken Soup for the Soul* series, America's #1 Success Coach, and featured teacher in the *The Secret*

"Mark and Takara have created a veritable feast of information for anyone wishing to discover and apply the law of attraction. It also includes some remarkable personal examples. I would say, without a doubt, this work contains the best explanation of this subject that I have ever read! If you are serious about utilizing the law of attraction in your life, this is a must-read for you."

- **Paul Stretton-Stephens**, Future Mindset Coach and Future Thinking Strategist

"For all those longing to transform their lives and open to a flow of authentic self-fulfillment *Unleash Your Future* is an inspiring and motivating must read! With their unique perspective Takara and Mark have taken the Law of Attraction a huge step further down the path to practical application helping to actuate our life's dreams. Beautifully written and easy to follow, it provides a fresh look at intentionally creating the lives we have always wanted."

- **Andi & Jonathan Goldman**, authors of *The Humming Effect: Sound Healing for Health and Happiness*

"Love this book as it provides the steps for what we can do in the present moment to create our future of prosperity. Straight forward and delivered in an authentic way."

- **Christopher Salem,** America's Prosperneur™

"Seriously, this is the LAST book that you will ever need to read. Takara and Mark have developed an extremely understandable and doable approach to FINALLY manifesting your dreams. The collaboration between the two of them is spectacular. Add this book to your 'need to read and IMPLEMENT' list."

- **Drs. Diane and Loren Mickelson,** creators of the *Mickelson Method*™

"After about a month working with Mark, I had 3 excellent job offers and more importantly, I had regained my confidence and had a toolbox to continue improving all aspects of my life. I can't thank Mark enough for his time, thoughtful guidance and inspiring model to help me be a better person."

- **Craig Hoosier,** Plant Operations Manager

"My life has changed so much *(since participating in Takara's manifesting classes)* ... I'm much happier ... when I was ready, it was only one or two days and this recruiter contacted me."

- **Shanti Devi**, Physicist, Poet, Priestess, Yogi, Marketeer

Takara Shelor is a passionate and skilled instructor. She provided us with several tools to bring clarity and light to our path and grow into our next level and reach our life purpose."

- **Beth Boyd Bell**, President, *FemCity Roanoke*

UNLEASH
Your
FUTURE

Maddy~
You can be, do, or experience
anything you can dream of. This
book will show you how. So dream
big Maddy! Good luck as
you embark on this new and
exciting phase of life.
                    Sincerely,
                    Mark Boldi

UNLEASH
YOUR
FUTURE

*The Powerful 5 Step Formula to
Transform Your Dreams Into Reality
Through the Law of Attraction*

Mark Boldizar
Takara Shelor

Forchianna Publishing
Radford, Virginia

Forchianna Publishing

Forchianna Publishing
P.O. Box 1363, Radford, VA 24143

Forchianna Publishing is a division of Forchianna L.L.C.

ISBN-10 0-9964310-3-9
ISBN-13 978-0-9964310-3-3

10 9 8 7 6 5 4 3 2 1
This book was typeset in Book Antiqua.

Dedication

We dedicate this book to you, the reader. Every word written and concept shared was with you in mind. May you glean much wisdom within these pages.

Acknowledgments

We'd like to thank AM, LM, and the New Science of Success Team. Without their help, this book would not exist. Gratitude also goes to our families and friends. Special thanks to our fabulous editor, Jeshua Hicks, and to Susie Carder, Amethyst Mahony, Derek Murphy, Jack Canfield, Lisa Wechtenhiser, Dave Chesson, Brad Pittis, and our students.

Table of Contents

List of Illustrations

Foreword

I was first introduced to the Law of Attraction in 1990. I was a young mother of two little girls struggling to figure out how to take care of them, pay my bills, and provide for my children.

I had joined a Multilevel marketing company, and they shared you can manifest anything you choose. It was a foreign concept for me and a bigger stretch to even imagine that was possible. Well, being that single mother of two, I needed to manifest a lot!

Growing up with a large family of 11, we were poor. So all I knew about manifesting was to get up earlier than the next kid so you could get a shower.

We grew up in lack and poverty. It taught me a lot. Manifesting and attracting anything I could ever dream wasn't in my lexicon.

My dad worked as a machinist, and my stepmom was a seamstress. What we knew was that there was always more month than money. Our goal was survival. We were lucky if we got three meals a day. That's what was normal in our reality.

So, this new way of thinking, and believing was exciting, and for the first time in my life I felt hope. Hope that my circumstances didn't dictate my outcome or my future. That anyone can create anything? That seemed like hocus-pocus!

The first book I read was *Think and Grow Rich by Napoleon Hill*. WOW, I could change my current reality with my thoughts. I became a student of this philosophy. I was hungry for anything that could help me change my current reality.

I became one of the top consultants in the MLM and won jewelry, cars, and cash. I was the top 10% of the company in under a year by implementing the practices that are laid out in this book.

I read *The Power of Now*, Eckert Tolle, *The Alchemist* by Paulo Coelho, *The Power of Positive Thinking* by Dr. Norman Vincent Peale. I became obsessed with how to change the patterns of my upbringing. Did you know that 80% of our emotional program is done by the time we are 8 years old? From 8 to 18 we have another 10%. And from 18 to death is another 10%. But that last 10% can change your life forever, it did mine!

I have gone on to build two 10-million-dollar companies and 7 other companies that have achieved the top 1.7% of money earners in the country. We have won multiple awards in both financial and entrepreneur achievements. I became an international speaker, consultant and award-winning author. With no more than my PHD, my public high school diploma! My education has been studying, implementing and taking radical action as laid out in one place, this book, *Unleash your Future!*

This book is about results, taking this conceptional topic and giving you specific actions backed by science and proven methodology. Mark and Takara have walked the walk and have done the research to show you how and why the technology works. Tools and strategy to implement, playing games to have you BELIEVE you too can experience manifesting simple things to more extravagant outcomes.

The choice is yours. Take the journey with us and discover for yourself what millions have been practicing for years. Implementation is the key to having all of your dreams manifest in front of you. Not thinking about it, not hoping it will work, but IMPLEMENTING it and being intentional about what you think about, what you talk about, so you can bring about your most profound future!

Your future starts here and now, just play along with Mark and Takara and see if your life is different after doing the exercises and being open to something different.

Become something bigger, bolder and braver. Isn't it time you live an extraordinary life? Isn't it your time and don't you deserve it? I think back to all those years ago, the power of one book, one conversation completely shifted my reality.

That scared single mom struggling became an icon in an industry because I believed in the unbelievable. If I can do it, you can too!

- **Susie Carder**, *Profit Coach, Bestselling Author*

Preface

Life can be a joy-filled epic adventure or a mundane experience of struggle, strife, and monotonous drudgery. The choice is entirely yours, and this book will help you make it.

Have you ever felt that something was missing? Something you know is important. Maybe you thought you knew what it was but had no idea how to bring the dream, the desire, the need, into reality. You tried everything you could think of, but nothing came of it. You lost hope and gave up.

Well, you didn't lose all hope, because you're reading this right now. That means some small ember of desire still burns. This book provides the perfect kindling to help that desire burst into a roaring flame where living the life of your dreams is made possible once more.

Maybe you've wanted to get a promotion or better job, have more money, enjoy a great romantic relationship, develop a better fit and healthy body, improve a skill, experience a better relationship with your kids, parents, co-workers, and/or friends. Perhaps, even having some of those things, you don't feel happy or fulfilled and continue to wish something would change.

Living the life of your dreams requires following a different roadmap *(or path)* than the one you've been on previously. It's a pathway of change, transformation, happiness, fulfillment, and goal achievement. *Unleash Your Future*, Book I of the New Science of Success Series takes you down that path.

Mark:

Ten years ago, I stumbled across a video containing information about a law that they say allows you to create your reality. As a scientist, I knew about many scientific laws. That there might be one I didn't know about caught my attention. It also brought up several questions:

Is this fantasy or is it real?

If The Law is real, then why didn't I learn about it in school or University?

If it's true that we create our reality, then why would I (or anyone) ever experience anything undesirable?

On and on the questions continued.

So there I was.

I just encountered a "law" I'd never heard of before, and most people I knew would dismiss as a hoax or the product of some snake-oil salesman.

I had a decision to make.

One you will also face.

Do I allow for the possibility that this law might exist and attempt to prove/disapprove it for myself? Or do I reject even the possibility, like almost everyone else I know most surely would?

It's not a straightforward decision.

Fortunately, I found myself highly intrigued by the idea of its potential existence and set out to learn more and test its validity for myself.

I ran into many roadblocks along the way. A mountain of information exists about it, yet nothing explained it in a way that I found useful when trying to apply it. I kept digging and kept being disappointed.

I kept at it, designing and carrying out my own experiments. Through trial and error, I began having more and more success in experiencing what I desired. I started with small things (as we recommend you do as well) and then worked my way up to manifesting the career of my dreams, making more money than ever before.

Along the way, a formula began to coalesce in my mind about the ingredients needed to bring a desire to fruition. I knew such a formula would help many people.

What I've come to understand and accept is that this Law is indeed real. And if it is real for me, then it is real for everyone, even if they don't believe in it. Universal principles and laws, by definition, apply to everyone.

———◆———

Takara:

When Mark approached me a few years ago to be his author success coach, he was unaware of my long-term interest and personal successes with The Law of Creation he was planning to write this book about.

I first learned about conscious creation, intentional manifestation, Law of Attraction, or the myriad of other names one can use when describing "getting what you want" through The Universal Law of Creation when I was putting myself through college. I was successful in utilizing it, even though I didn't know how or why it worked.

Since then I've had some incredible successes creating my reality including several sports cars, living on a million-dollar yacht in Fiji and the South Pacific for a while, becoming a bestselling author several times, having my son's college education completely paid for, and much more.

Yet, things didn't always work out as planned, and in certain areas of my life, I had difficulty manifesting. If I'd known then what I know now, things could have been so much easier even in those areas. And that is my wish for you. That by learning the things available to you in this book, you'll be able to create the reality you desire in a much easier, less stressful way.

I was thrilled when Mark started sharing with me his formula for working with this law and the things he'd learned about how it works. And I knew that a couple of additional steps were vital to truly achieve your dreams. I also realized that over the past 25 years I'd been learning how to fine-tune and successfully work with each of the components in the formula.

I knew about all the necessary ingredients. I just didn't know how to put them together properly and consistently until Mark came along with his information and we got fully immersed in how it all works.

Eventually, he asked if I'd like to join him in creating this teaching. I responded with a resounding, "yes," and *The New Science of Success* was born.

———◆———

Introduction

Every human is born with precisely the abilities they need to lead a happy, fulfilling, successful life. Yet few recognize those innate abilities and fewer still know how to use them to their fullest potential. We designed this book to help you do both.

Unleash Your Future offers a completely fresh look at intentional creation … providing an actual formula that explains not only how to program the Universe but also when attempts fail, it pinpoints precisely what went wrong and what you can do about it.

There is a fundamental, universal law that governs the experiences you have in life. It's often called The Law of Attraction or LOA for short. We prefer to call it the *Universal Law of Creation* or simply *The Law*.

Most people have never heard of this law and certainly never learned about it in any science class. But that doesn't mean it doesn't exist. Humans lived for thousands of years before discovering electricity. And yet, it was here all along. Once discovered, human ingenuity created formulae and systems to harness electricity's power for everyone's benefit. Similarly, our formula and systems help you harness the power of The Law to achieve your goals, dreams, and aspirations.

For millennia, The Law has been recognized, understood, used, and taught by various individuals, cultures, and philosophies. In more recent times, a plethora of books, movies, and internet websites have talked about it. Yet, the resulting library of information offers little practical guidance about how to use The Law to your benefit.

Upon first learning about this law, you'll most likely have questions and possibly doubts. This book will help provide the answers you seek, and attempt to dispel any doubts that may arise along the way.

Our intention is to help you better understand The Law and teach you how to conduct your own experiments. From there, you can draw your own conclusions about its validity.

We've laid out the formula in an easy to follow step-by-step fashion that will help you test it yourself. We have every confidence that by understanding the formula and diligently working on the various components it contains, you can achieve the success you're been longing for.

Besides providing you with a thorough and systematic approach to understanding The Law, we've woven our personal stories and many metaphors throughout to help you better understand.

We chose not to explore the deep scientific theories on how The Law turns thoughts into physical reality. Once you understand the formula and know how to use it, you probably won't care about all the details behind "how" it actually works.

You don't need to have a Ph.D. in electrical engineering to know how to flip a light switch to "on." The same is true for successfully mastering The Law. Once you know how to "program the Universe," the rest becomes much less important.

The frustrations around working with The Law, which most people seem to run into while learning about it, almost universally stem from the presentation being far too theoretical. Few teachings, books, movies, discussions get into the specifics about how to precisely and consistently program The Law to achieve your dreams, goals, and desires. Fewer still discuss the additional steps needed to bring your desires into reality. We've not found anything anywhere that shows people how to analyze what needs to change when things don't go as planned. This book teaches you:

- the critical components needed to program The Law
- numerous ways to improve your use of each aspect of the formula
- the additional steps necessary to bring a desire into fruition
- a method to analyze a failed attempt so you can have greater success the next time

We wrote this book from our (Mark and Takara's) unique perspectives working with The Law. Each of our stories builds one upon the other to show you how we came to understand and use The Law to our advantage.

Our intention in sharing these stories is not to brag, but to offer examples of how we have worked with The Law to spark ideas of how you can use it yourself. Through our intentional engagement of The Law, we unlocked its secrets and wish to share those secrets with you ... *so you too can have outstanding success.*

This book guides you on a journey toward what you want to have, do, and experience, but previously thought was impossible. We bring forth our own experiences so you understand it isn't a magic "manifest a million dollars instantly" machine, but a tool that takes dedication and effort to master.

This framework is not the only one that exists. Many successful people throughout history have found their own path. But those people were truly dedicated to their desires. They worked tirelessly for years to achieve their goals. Failure was never an option. And, inadvertently, they ended up using several elements we will discuss here, even if they wouldn't have called them "The Law" or even been aware that such a concept exists.

Through our stories, you will more fully understand how The Law works and how you can use it to create more health, wealth, success, better relationships, and greater happiness just as we have. We hope you take what you learn here and manifest even greater things.

Our explanation of The Law contains no gimmicks, no promises of effortless manifesting, no "ours is the only way" programs, and no BS. What we've discovered is the essence of how The Law works distilled into a simple systematic approach with a super simple equation that makes it easy to understand and remember.

As we walk you through the process of understanding step by step, imagine yourself taking the journey with us.

There are no limits on what is possible with The Law. It's normal to not believe that yet. Once you decide to follow the formula and experiment with it for yourself, your confidence will grow with each level of success you achieve.

We know there are many reasons you haven't reached all your goals yet: self-doubt; others telling you it's not possible; life's circumstances blindsiding you and ripping away your dreams. We've been there ourselves, and so have many others. So set all of that aside for now.

If humans always gave up when things got tough, we'd still be hunter-gatherers migrating from cave to cave. It's through tenacity, conscious effort, and clear direction that you can achieve the things you want most. This book helps you with all of that and more.

Unfortunately, many of us have been led to believe that:

- success and happiness are meant for others, but not us,
- we don't deserve the things we desire, or

- we should be ashamed that we even want them.

Those beliefs simply aren't true. You deserve the success you crave. No one will give it to you for free, however. You must make it for yourself.

Unleash Your Future offers a fresh look at intentional creation. It offers a map for you to go from desire to fruition. But you must be willing to put in the work to make those changes happen.

We know you can achieve your dreams. Our stories show it's possible. We also share stories of others who had to overcome many obstacles to attain their goals. If they can do it, so can you. As you progress through this journey of learning to manifest, experiencing greater and greater achievements along the way, we and the world are waiting to hear your stories of success.

You are a powerful creator, limited only by what you believe is possible. Open your mind, set aside your preconceived notions about how life works, let us take you by the hand and lead you on this journey to discover the secrets to success that you've been seeking.

In the Beginning ...

Developing an understanding of The Law of Creation (The Law) is like climbing a mountain. As we guide you step by step along this journey, you might begin a far distance from your goals (the top of the mountain). With each revelation (resulting in a shift in perception and behavior) you move ever upward, getting closer and closer to achieving the things you want most.

Your current understanding of The Law likely differs from someone else's understanding because what you've studied and your life experiences have been different. Since we have to start somewhere, we decided to start at the proverbial foot of the mountain ... *the beginning*.

You are already creating every moment of every day. Each one of your life experiences begins with a thought. Then you add in a few other ingredients (discussed in great depth throughout this book) and the Universe acts on those to create your various life experiences. The conversion of thought into life experience is known as the Universal Law of Creation ... *often called The Law of Attraction or LOA for short*.

This law is as fundamental to life on our planet as the law of gravity. You never really think about or question the existence of gravity. But you know it is always at work because you wake up each morning still firmly on the ground … *just like you have been every day of your life.*

The law of gravity is always operating, even when you're not thinking about it. Because you learned about it in school and you've observed that objects don't randomly float away, you accept that the law of gravity exists and is always in effect.

Similarly, by studying and experimenting with The Universal Law of Creation, we've concluded that this law is also real and always in effect.

But unlike the universally accepted law of gravity, most people don't accept, believe, or understand The Universal Law of Creation. It's not something taught in school and is often marginalized by those in the scientific community.

New Concepts Are Historically Disregarded

Lack of widespread acceptance of principles that don't conform to the scientific paradigms of the day has been common throughout history. Copernicus and Galileo proposed a radical new theory in the 16th and 17th centuries. Their theory was that the sun was the center of the solar system and that the earth revolved around the sun. The paradigm of the day, supported by the church, was that the earth was the center of the universe. The Inquisition persecuted Galileo for his new proposed scientific theory.

You learned in school that Copernicus and Galileo were correct, that the earth does indeed revolve around the sun. You also learned that the earth is round, even though during the time of Columbus many believed it was flat. Columbus didn't fall off the edge of the earth when he set off on his journey to sail around the world.

Modern times are not immune to the firm grip of established beliefs and paradigms. The current scientific community has no room for a new theory that proposes you are the center of the universe; that you have the power to create any life experience you desire.

Yet every significant discovery and innovation comes from a mind willing to think outside the box of what is "normal," understood, and acceptable in any field.

You might also have trouble believing, or even considering the possibility, that a Universal Law of Creation exists.

You are not alone.

The implications of this law are so powerful and far-reaching that it is understandable that your first reaction might be something like, "No way. This can't be true!"

You are reading this book, however, which means you didn't stop there. You must have followed that initial reaction with, "But what if it is?"

The idea is quite intriguing, isn't it?

You, like everyone else who first comes face-to-face with this proposed new creative principle, have to make an important initial decision. Do you reject this proposal because it doesn't fit your current thoughts and beliefs about how life works? Or do you allow for the possibility that it may exist?

If you decide The Law is possible.
Then what?

Your Personal Journey with The Law

Beginning your journey exploring The Law isn't necessarily easy. It can be lonely. You may know very few people who believe this law might be real.

This journey of discovering if there is such a law and how it works can also seem overwhelming. If you do an online search for "The Law of Attraction," you will quickly be overrun with information.

While it may feel encouraging that so much information exists about this law, you soon discover that the information differs from source to source with few commonly accepted general principles or terms. One source may say that a particular thing is the most important. Another source says something else entirely. You can quickly become buried in far too much information.

Mark knows the feeling because he was there. The only common themes he could find were so theoretical that they didn't help advance his research and understanding. He found a few commonalities like "thoughts become things," "you are what you think," and "think, believe, receive." While these general statements would be true if The Law were real, they do little to help you make that decision for yourself.

Great Previous Works

While it's true that there is a lot of information available about The Law, there are some works that have been around for some time and have more history and credibility. These works differ in their approach and how they're written, yet we felt it was important that you be aware of them.

Mark:

During my 10+ years of study and experimentation, I explored an abundance of unique books, movies, and internet writings on the topic. Some information that resonated most with me includes:

- *Think and Grow Rich* by Napoleon Hill
- *The Science of Mind* by Ernest Holmes
- *The Law of Attraction* by Esther and Jerry Hicks (The Teachings of Abraham)
- *As a Man Thinketh* by James Allen
- The many writings of Neville Goddard
- The movie *The Secret*

Think and Grow Rich was a book that I read very early in my search for understanding.[1] Napoleon Hill wrote the book from a very relatable perspective. He described how regular people use The Law to create remarkable success.

While it was difficult for me to find a simple, practical approach to engaging The Law in the book, the credible real-life examples of people using The Law were compelling. They helped to solidify my belief in the possibility of The Law's existence.

Someone Hill wrote about struck a very personal cord. Charles Schwab became a very successful steel executive in the early half of the 20th century. Hill described Schwab using The Law to rise to a level of extraordinary success at Bethlehem Steel, one of the largest steel companies of the time.

Schwab's story resonated with me deeply because I already knew a great deal about him before reading the book.

Charles Schwab grew up in a small town in western Pennsylvania called Loretto. After becoming successful, he built an immense mansion there.

My great grandmother was an immigrant from Ireland who came to Loretto and worked for Charles Schwab at his estate. My mother was born and raised in Loretto. I was born and raised only miles from there. I visited Loretto often to see my grandparents. Those visits often included walking around the beautiful gardens of the Schwab estate.

Loretto is also home to Saint Francis University, formally St. Francis College, which I attended just as Schwab had done.

I used to play golf at Immergrün Golf Club, which Schwab built. The golf course is a unique nine-hole course designed with most holes curving out and to the left to accommodate Schwab's slice. My grandfather told me stories about the building of the course and how he used to caddie there when he was young. He describes how Schwab would golf there with his rich friends and business associates.

My personal connection with Schwab helped me to identify with the successes in Hill's book in a very real and tangible way. I can remember reading Schwab's example and thinking to myself, "Hey, I know who that guy is and what some of his life must've looked like. "

The movie, *The Secret*, also affected my acceptance of The Law as not only plausible but also most likely probable.[2] There were many examples of people creating extraordinary success by using The Law. This movie brought to life the concepts I had already been reading about in books.

I then discovered *The Science of Mind* by Ernest Holmes.[3] His work combined eastern and western teaching, philosophies, and religious concepts into a unified understanding of how the universe works along with the role and power of the individual in this universe. For me, *The Science of Mind* turned the seemingly fantastical possibility of The Law, or "The Thing Itself" as Holmes put it, into a proposed scientific principle that could be understood, studied, and experimented with just like all other accepted scientific principles.

As a trained scientist experienced in practically applying other scientific principles in corporate environments, *The Science of Mind* helped me see how I could experiment with The Law in a way similar to how I'd been experimenting with other scientific concepts throughout my career. Holmes was clear that just reading about the concepts was not enough. It required actual experimentation.

I had a profound sense that Holmes was correct in his teachings. I also knew that personal experimentation in the living laboratory of my life was necessary to provide the personal proof required for me to move from considering the Universal Law of Creation a plausible theory to a certain scientific principle.

Takara:

For me, studying and experimenting with The Law began long before I even knew it was a law or that it had a name.

While in college, I read an article in a professional woman's business magazine talking about how to create a vision board to help in achieving success.

Remember, this was a very long time ago. Vision boards are widely talked about and accepted now. But at the time, I'd never heard of them. And it sounded like one of the most ridiculous ideas I'd ever heard. I thought, "How could cutting out a bunch of pictures and pasting them on a board possibly do anything toward achieving one's goals?" To say I was skeptical would be a major understatement. Yet this magazine was my authority on all things related to career success, so I followed the instructions despite my immense skepticism.

I was madly in love, so I included a picture of my boyfriend along with some beautiful wedding rings I found in a magazine somewhere. My dad was a mechanical engineer with an intense passion for cars and racing that began when he was a small child. He even built and designed a race car that a team ran on a local track, winning several trophies along the way. Even though I cared little for racing myself, I did really like the look and sleek lines of a beautiful and fast car. I found a photo of a gold RX7 ... a car I'd never seen on the road anywhere, but that looked gorgeous in the magazine I was searching through. So I put that on my board. I also included an image of a tropical beach with very white sand and gorgeous ocean water, plus a pile of cash.

About a year later, when I was breaking up with my fiancé, I took down the vision board and forgot all about it.

I'd had my new car for about two weeks when it suddenly hit me one day while driving .... "wait a minute, I used to have a picture of this car on my wall." It was a gorgeous, and "oh my goodness" fast, gold RX7. I thought about the vision board poster and the images I'd placed on there. Gold RX7 ... check.

I had broken off the engagement with the guy I'd had on the board and we did, in fact, have wedding rings when I broke up with him. We were planning a wedding and had even been looking for a house …. check.

He and I had taken an incredible trip to Miami Beach for spring break. Sandy beach, palm trees, gorgeous ocean … check.

I was driving an RX7 and putting myself through college. I'd obviously manifested enough money to do all that … check.

I was flabbergasted. I didn't understand the first thing about why it worked, only that it very obviously did.

One by one, each of the dreams on the board had come true. It changed my life. It even changed my career choice. I was pursuing a career in business at the time, but what I really wanted was to be an Industrial Engineer. I just didn't believe that was possible for me. This silly vision board exercise made me realize that absolutely anything is possible. Why would I want to settle for goals that weren't really what I wanted? So I applied to one of the top 10 engineering schools in the nation and made that dream happen as well.

A few years into my engineering career, I was having a lot of health challenges and found an MLM (Multi-Level Marketing / Network Marketing) product that made a huge positive difference. Because it helped me so much, I became a distributor to, hopefully, help others with their health as well. One of the first things I remember them saying about being successful was to read *Think and Grow Rich* by Napoleon Hill.[4] With my dad's car obsession, I grew up hearing about Henry Ford, and his inclusion in the book made it seem more real and relatable for me personally, much like Mark's story of the connection with Charles Schwab had done for him.

Someone introduced me to the work of Esther and Jerry Hicks when I was in my early 30s. They are the ones who made the words "Law of Attraction" popular in American culture. I began listening to talks and reading many books and articles by New Thought teachers from the past like Neville Goddard, Catherine Ponder, James Allen, W. Clement Stone, Wallace Wattles, William Walker Atkinson, and more. I became an avid student of Stuart Wilde and his teachings around *Affirmations, Miracles,* and personal empowerment. I loved Shakti Gawain's book on *Creative Visualization.*[5] Many years later, someone gave me a copy of the original version of the movie, *The Secret,* which included Esther Hicks. Since then, I've enjoyed many other books, movies, articles, and audios on the subject.

I've been teaching private clients and groups about vision boards, goal achievement, personal empowerment, and life transformation for over two decades. Many of my students have had great success with The Law.

---◆---

Exercise:

You'll want to start a notebook/journal related to your knowledge gained and the experiments you do while working with The Law.

Jot down any insights you had while reading this chapter.

List any books, audios, videos, etc. that you have studied previously about conscious creation or LOA.

Key Concepts:

- The Law is not widely known and understood.
- New proposed laws often take years, decades, or even longer to be accepted by the scientific establishment of the day.
- A few helpful books and videos already exist, but they don't really explain how to work effectively with The Law.

The Past Leaves Clues

Before embarking on a journey, it's often important to find out more about where you're going, and it's even better if you can talk to someone who has already been there. We've been on this journey ourselves, and we've helped many others navigate it successfully.

Our personal journeys have been vastly different as we've each learned to work with The Law. That means we can offer you different approaches and perspectives to try so you can determine what works best or resonates most with you as you do your own experimenting.

Takara

To understand why my approach to working with The Law is of a more intuitive nature than the more scientific step-by-step experimental method that Mark has experienced, you need to know a little about my past. My background was fairly rough. Experiencing physical abuse and severe bullying are just two of the many unpleasant things I had to contend with growing up.

What resulted was an unhealthy need to be the best at whatever I was doing and yet always being terrified it wouldn't last. As you will learn later, whatever you focus on you create and expectations have consequences. I always excelled, and those successes were always followed by something going terribly awry.

My engineering management career was exceedingly stressful. One day it was just too much. I had a complete mental/emotional meltdown. It was then that flashbacks of being raped flooded in. It was an experience I had successfully suppressed for 15 years. I laid on the floor in the fetal position sobbing uncontrollably for several hours. Thank heavens I was at home and not at work.

I quickly got some much needed psychological help. Rather than looking at that moment as horrible, I saw it as a ray of hope and an opportunity for serious change. Now I understood why I was so unhappy ... *I'd been stuffing negative experiences and emotions for decades.* No one is ever truly perfect, yet I always thought I had to be ... *at absolutely everything.*

Something amazing happened when those terrible memories surfaced. It was as if someone had found my "intuition switch" and flipped it to the "on" position. I suddenly "knew" to visit a particular store, purchase a certain book, have private sessions with various alternative health professionals, and take specific classes. It turns out that in suppressing the deeply traumatizing memory of being raped, I had also suppressed one skill we all innately have that is vitally important in manifesting ... *our intuition.*

After discovering the joys and benefits of journaling and meditation, I made a radical shift. I had been miserable and far too stressed in the corporate world. So I mustered up the courage to quit my job, move to an island, and co-found a non-profit for dolphins and whales. Finding true happiness and a life of meaning and purpose became my quest.

Over a period of years, using many techniques including some I developed myself, I addressed and healed many of the emotional wounds. I also found ways to manage stress, fine-tune and enhance intuition, gain clarity and inner peace. I learned to look for and follow subtle signs.

—◆—

As you will discover in a later chapter, developing intuition will become more and more important as you work with The Law. Mark's approach to working with The Law uses science paired with intuition. Takara's primary approach is to use intuition paired with logic. Both approaches are highly effective. As we mentioned before, by offering both we will help you find the method that works best for you.

—◆—

Wisdom Gained

Mark:

As I contemplated the potential validity of this law, it occurred to me that if it existed; it had to exist throughout my life. Even if I was not consciously aware of The Law, I should be able to find examples where it was at work.

Looking back and reviewing my personal history, one experience stood out as potential proof. It was an experience I had while working in Europe. My role was to help manufacturing plants become more efficient and lower their cost to produce products resulting in the company's profits going up. My formula for success was applying fundamental scientific principles to improve processes and profitability in a measurable and sustainable way.

It was relatively early in my career. Most of the significant developments and improvements in the company occurred through a more empirical, experience-based approach to problem-solving. Several scientists had worked for the company for decades, accumulating knowledge about how the processes worked. Their experiential wisdom was difficult to teach to others. This approach also led to these experienced scientists being held in high regard as "experts." They had little incentive to teach others what they knew, as that might jeopardize their exclusive expert status.

As I touched on earlier, throughout history science has been no stranger to resisting alternative theories that challenge currently held paradigms. That was the position I found myself in.

They tasked me with reducing product costs. A potentially fruitful area of investigation was to substitute a new lower-cost ingredient for the higher-priced one currently being used. Such a change could compromise none of the product's physical properties, level of quality, or any other aspect of the product or process.

My investigation led me to an alternative material that might replace one of the principal ingredients. This new material, if successfully substituted, would lead to millions of dollars in savings. I was very excited to pursue the possibility.

I started with the fundamental scientific principles at the heart of how this product was manufactured, plus the resultant properties valued most by the customers who bought it. The fundamental science supported that this new material should/would work. I went over my analysis with a former mentor in the company who agreed with my conclusions. This gave me even more confidence that shifting to this new material would be doable.

My proposal for testing the new material ran into a major roadblock. The older, experience-based scientists disagreed. Previously someone had tried the new material I was proposing. They had concluded that it couldn't work.

Here I was, the young scientist meeting the enormous wall of resistance. It would've been easier if I'd just deferred to the more experienced scientists and moved on to something else. However, my belief in the science made me press on with the idea.

Luckily, I had previously developed the trust of one of the plant managers in Europe. I explained to him why I thought this new material would work and showed him my analysis. He agreed to let me run a trial at his plant. I remember feeling so excited about being given this opportunity. Yet I was also feeling some doubt. My reputation and future career were literally on the line.

To alleviate the doubt, I reviewed the science again and again. As I prepared for the plant trial, I created a rational plan and a clear picture of what I expected to happen during the trial. I remember having so much passion and excitement going in, along with a high level of confidence that the trial would play out just as I had planned and envisioned.

The day of the trial finally arrived. The plant prepared just as I had instructed. I followed the new material from the prep stage through to the finished product. As the final product properties and quality requirements were being measured, I could feel the butterflies in my stomach as I waited anxiously for the results.

One by one the test results were measured and recorded. Each of the product requirements was met with flying colors. The reality began to sink in. This trial was a resounding success. This new material, which was deemed unacceptable by other scientists, actually worked just as I had envisioned and believed it would. My thought/idea, powered by my unbridled passion and belief, became a reality. I experienced in real life what I had imagined.

This memory gave me a wonderful example of The Law at work. It offered an immense piece of evidence that increased my belief in the possibility of The Law. I was rushing forward toward believing that it was both real and universal.

Exercise:

Jot down any insights you've gained reading this chapter.

Think about your personal history and try to uncover one or more experiences where you can see that The Law was operating in your life. That may include negative experiences.

Write about those in your journal or notebook. The more experiments you do that have successful results (including memories from the past), the greater your confidence will be in The Law and your ability to consciously program it.

Key Concepts

- The Law has always existed ... even when you were unaware of it.
- Upon reflection, you will find evidence of The Law at work in your own life.
- Finding personal examples will build your confidence in starting to intentionally experiment with The Law.

You Are Not Alone

Many well-known and highly successful people had to overcome limiting beliefs and the negative opinion of others to succeed. We teach you how to do that in later chapters. Some took years to bring their dreams into reality.

Sylvester Stallone was rejected over a 1000 times by talent scouts, agents, and others in the film industry as he tried to get a job as an actor. He even had to sell his dog to pay the electric bill and eventually became homeless. Despite these severe challenges, he never gave up. He wrote the script for Rocky, played the lead and it ended up grossing $225 million at the box office launching his career. He says, "I take rejection as someone blowing a bugle in my ear to wake me up and get going, rather than retreat."[6]

Oprah came from extreme poverty, was abused as a child, and ran away from home at 13.[7] She was fired from a Baltimore TV station for being "unfit for television news."[8] She went on to host The Oprah Winfrey Show for 25 seasons. It won 47 Daytime Emmy Awards.[9] Her career also includes acting in movies. She was the first North-American black multi-billionaire.[10]

JJ Watt is considered one of the best defensive ends in the NFL. When he first went to college at Central Michigan, they saw him as a tight end and not a defensive end. He left Central Michigan and walked on at Wisconsin as a defensive end. He earned a scholarship and was later drafted into the NFL.[11]

Lisa Nichols, one of the world's most requested motivational speakers, was told in college by both her writing and speaking professors she should never speak and she should never write. She is now a self-made millionaire.[12]

Michael Jordan, when trying out for the varsity high school basketball team, was assigned to the junior varsity team ... *which left him in tears.*[13] He turned out to be one of the greatest basketball players of all time. In his own words, "I've missed more than 9000 shots in my career. I've lost almost 300 games. 26 times I've been trusted to take the game-winning shot and missed. I've failed over and over and over again in my life. And that is why I succeed."[14]

Albert Einstein didn't speak until he was 4 years old.[15] He failed his entrance exam to college. His father died considering his son a failure. He later developed the theory of relativity and did groundbreaking work in physics and math and won a Nobel Prize in Physics in 1921.[16]

Eddie Hall was expelled from school at 14 and began working out at the gym.[17] Before that, he had been on course to become an Olympic swimmer. Being expelled and no longer on the swim team left him deeply depressed. At his father's urging, he starting working out. After his first competition, he declared that he would be the World's Strongest Man. He promised his Nan (grandmother) on her deathbed that he would win that title.[18] He did in 2017 and was the first person to deadlift 500 kg (1,102 lbs).[19]

Charles Darwin said in his autobiography, "I was considered by all my masters (school teachers) and my father, a very ordinary boy, rather below the common standard of intellect." He was considered a failure and dropped out of college more than once. He later became "one of the most influential scientific minds of our time."[20]

Lady Gaga was bullied so badly that she didn't even want to go to school sometimes. In college, a group of students started a Facebook group whose sole purpose was to bash her. She is the "only woman in history to have won a BAFTA, Golden Globe, Grammy and Oscar in the same year."[21]

Allan Scott, producer of the highly successful Queen's Gambit tv show, said it took 30 years and nine rewrites before it finally aired. Every studio he approached said no one would be interested in chess.[22]

Abraham Lincoln had one defeat, loss, or failure after another. He lost his job at age 23. At age 26, the love of his life died. He lost many elections at the state and federal level. Refusing to give up despite so many obstacles, he was eventually elected President of the United States.[23]

We're sure you've heard of many more.

The moral of these stories is that success means never giving up and the necessity of believing in yourself and your dreams even when those around you don't.

We gave you so many examples here to show that it's not just a fluke. It's not just that one "special person" who can achieve their dreams. None of these people achieved what they wanted by doing nothing. They dragged themselves out of the mud, believed they could do it, and put in the hard work to get there, even if it took years. It can be that regular kid down the street who had abusive parents or the one who did poorly in school. It can be the destitute artist with nothing to their name. It can also be you experiencing great success.

Exercise:

Jot down in your journal any insights you've gained while reading this chapter.

Think about other examples of people who overcame obstacles to manifest extraordinary success. Write about them in your journal.

Do you find any of their stories motivating? If so, put a brief note somewhere that says, "If ____ can succeed, I can too." Or choose words that resonate with you more.

Have you ever experienced someone telling you that you would never achieve something or you weren't good enough to experience something? Reflect on how it made you feel and write about it in your journal. What did you do because of that person's opinion? Did you prove them wrong or did you believe them and let it destroy your dreams?

Key Concepts

- There are lots of people who became successful even though they faced setback after setback.
- It's best to not let the negative opinion of others fill you with doubt.
- The only person truly standing in your way is you.

Bumps in the Road

Getting to the place where you not only accept The Law as real but have mastered programming it to consistently reap the rewards can be a deeply personal and unique journey. Along the way, there are likely to be many highs and lows, successes and setbacks. You may have to undergo quite a few do-overs to get it right.

You can read all about The Law and listen to stories of countless others who have used it successfully. Yet your own experiences will have a far greater impact on your understanding and mastery of it.

Finding examples in your past can be a brilliant start in attaining belief. But genuine success begins when you can program The Law in the "now" and achieve the goal or desire you intended.

Accepting The Law as real is not the end of the journey. It's just the beginning. Before acceptance, you were simply driving toward the mountain. Only after acceptance is it time to begin your climb.

Once accepted, you then get to ponder the huge implications of what that means. You have to come to terms with the realization that you are the architect of your life and it's up to you what you program into The Law. Life can happen to you or you can make it happen.

It's beneficial to know the emotional stages people can experience with any life change since most people go through all of them at about this point in their journey.

Even accepting the possibility of The Law can challenge your most fundamental beliefs about life. Like any change, either positive or negative, going through the five emotional stages of mourning (change/grief) is inevitable.

You might wonder, "Why would I experience grief over accepting The Law as real?"

It happens because you are suddenly mourning the loss of one of the strongest anchor points you've had. You may have thought life simply happened to you. With awareness of The Law, you learn that you are the primary driving force behind it.

To accept The Law as real, you must pull up that anchor and set sail for a destination completely unknown. It forces you way outside your comfort zone and can evoke an immense sense of loss accompanied by strong, unpleasant emotions. The amount of emotional turmoil that begins to churn within can be monumental.

Discovering that your own thoughts and beliefs played a major role in your previous experiences can be staggering. Realizing you are the designer of your life experience represents a significant shift in your perception of everything.

That can be viewed as both a blessing and a curse (*not really*). The blessing is that if you have that much influence on the circumstances of your life, then you have the opportunity to change the parts of it you don't like. On the other hand, it means you have to take a great deal more responsibility for your thoughts, words, and actions. And for many, particularly those who aren't used to paying attention, that can be a daunting task.

You may be aware that people grieve when they lose a loved one. But grief or mourning can happen with many other life experiences including moving to a new location, getting married or divorced, being diagnosed with cancer or some other illness, watching as your child heads off for the first time to grade school or college, and many more.

Understanding these stages of change and looking at the emotions you may have already been experiencing, and are likely to continue to experience as you grow and change throughout life, is very important and will greatly assist you.

In 1969 Elisabeth Kübler-Ross laid out the five stages of grief[24]:

- Denial
- Anger
- Bargaining
- Depression
- Acceptance

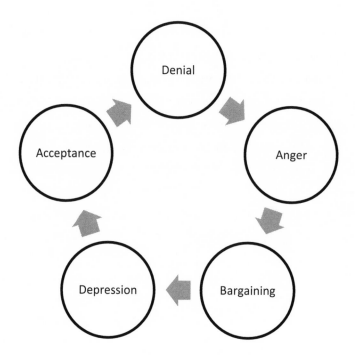

Figure 1. Five Stages of Grief

Others have suggested that there are more stages to the grieving process. Yet these five do a marvelous job of explaining the stages we've experienced and that Takara has helped countless clients face as they deal with various life changes and situations.

To ultimately become comfortable working with The Law, acceptance is required. That is the last stage of the process. On your way there, you will most likely go through some, possibly all, of the other stages. They can happen in any order. Understanding a bit more about each stage and how each may look related to your acceptance of The Law will help you better navigate this part of your manifesting journey.

If you don't fully feel and move through each of these emotions, you can get firmly stuck in one and never move beyond it. That applies to not only acceptance of The Law but any life change. We'll discuss in a later chapter why positive emotion is so important in intentional creation.

Denial

Denial is the first stage you are likely to encounter. In dealing with any change or loss, the first step is to pretend it isn't happening or didn't happen. It's much like being in shock ... *you go numb and refuse to deal with whatever is screaming for your attention.* Even after a tremendous loss of a loved one, a job, or something else equally devastating, some people have to go on about their day as if nothing has changed to cope with the devastation.

The denial phase can take as little as a few minutes or as much as several years. Takara was so stuck in denial over the trauma of her rape experience that it was 15 years before she even remembered that it happened. It's a powerful protection mechanism that prevents us from experiencing emotional pain until we are ready. However, as Takara shared, it also prevented her from accessing her intuition.

Before you were aware of The Law, you most likely didn't take responsibility for the less than positive experiences in your life. So, your immediate reaction might be a complete denial of The Law's existence when you first hear about it. You may think, "I would never create the experiences I don't like. That's ridiculous."

There's no escaping the unpleasantness of coming to terms with The Law being real all the time. Gravity is not a sometimes principle. You don't stick to the earth one day and float away the next. So, to fully accept The Law means you also have to accept your role as the creator of your life experience.

That isn't to say you create absolutely everything. Sometimes life truly does just happen. But more often than not you create most of what you experience:

- the turmoil with your significant other
- the new job with the big salary increase
- the car breakdown because you ignored the tell-tell signs it needed repair
- the new friendship you enjoy

As children, we're taught that throwing fits of anger or crying in public are not socially acceptable behaviors. As adults, we buy into the idea that negative emotion is something we should avoid. Rather than learning and developing healthy coping mechanisms to feel the emotions fully in a constructive way and completely let them go, we often develop avoidance tactics stuffing the emotions somewhere within or we go into fits of rage at unexpected and inappropriate times.

Anger is often a response to feeling powerless. Even when you're not aware of why you're angry, feeling like there's nothing you can do to stop or change a situation often causes anger to rise within.

———◆———

Takara

I first learned about these stages and some effective ways to deal with them while facing the traumatic rape memory that I mentioned previously.

It was terrifying going through the intense emotions that surfaced unexpectedly along with the memories. I'd become a master at stuffing powerful emotion and never once allowed myself to feel seriously angry or sad. I found not being able to stop crying or prevent going into a rage was extremely distressing. I felt out of control.

Thank heavens I had help. Besides several visits to a psychologist where I learned the importance of journaling and was told about several excellent books to read, I also began seeing a spiritual counselor/energy healer week after week who helped me more than words can express.

Synchronicity also played a major role in my healing of this deep wound. Intuition and synchronicity go hand in hand in manifesting and following the signs. There is no way I could have imagined how these two events would come together.

A few years before the memories surfaced, Working Women Magazine had a big weekend event in Manhattan, and I invited my best friend to go with me.

We loved visiting "The City" and were always on the lookout for reasons to do so.

Multiple speakers were lecturing on various topics at the event. I don't remember what the title of the lecture was or why I attended, but the book by the author giving the lecture would later become a key to my recovery. The book was *When Smart People Fail* by Carole Hyatt and Linda Gottleb. I'm sure that wasn't the name of the lecture, as I probably wouldn't have attended if it was. I hadn't yet realized that I felt like a failure even though I was highly successful as most people define success.

When everything in my life fell apart, the memories surfaced and extreme emotions began running amuck. Amid all that, I suddenly remembered the lecture and the book. Luckily, I could find it at a local bookstore. It was years before buying books online became popular.

Synchronicity (some might call it Divine intervention) had me attend a lecture I didn't yet know I needed in order to heal a deep wound I didn't yet know I had.

The more intense the situation, the stronger the emotions can be. Your emotional rollercoaster associated with accepting The Law is unlikely to be anywhere near the intensity Takara described above.

Anger

You may not like the notion that you are responsible for what you experience. Your dislike may bubble into anger with many causes:

- why didn't anyone teach you about The Law,
- does The bloody Law even exist,
- could you have avoided certain unpleasant experiences if you'd only known about The Law sooner?

It's perfectly normal to have those thoughts, and most of us experience them to varying degrees. It's important that you fully face and explore any anger that arises so you can process it, release it, and move on.

Finding a healthy way to express your anger, rather than aiming it at other people, is important. Some like to get all the words out on paper, journaling their way through the emotional pain. Others go for a run or strenuous hike. Dancing, kickboxing, punching a heavy bag, and even screaming help others. Find a way that can work for you and use it whenever necessary.

Bargaining

When dealing with change or grief, the bargaining phase is you trying to "wheel and deal" with the Universe and convince yourself of something that feels better than dealing with the truth. It is an attempt to make everything OK when clearly things are not. It is the almost nonsensical notion that somehow if you do, acquire, or say a certain thing, then everything will magically be alright ... *even if things are a complete disaster at the moment.* For situations of loss, that often looks like going on a shopping spree, losing a certain amount of weight, or getting a new boyfriend or girlfriend. The thought goes like this, "If I only get this dress (car, etc.), then everything will be OK" Or, "If I just lose these 10 pounds, everything will be OK."

As you wrestle with the idea of The Law's existence, when bargaining shows up you may say something like, "Well maybe I created this experience (one I like), but other experiences happen some other way." You are bargaining to only take responsibility for the good stuff. Some events that happen are outside our control as we've already mentioned. But many directly result from our mindset, which influences our actions.

People are bargaining when they talk about "using" LOA to manifest something they want. It's as if they believe The Law to be a magic wand you can pull out of your pocket and use only when you want to. Or it's a great vending machine in the sky that can be turned on and off at will.

There is no half measure with The Law. It is universal, and bargaining for something less than universal is futile. But as with the other stages, it is perfectly normal to go through bargaining as you head along the path to full acceptance.

Depression

Depression is a stage in which you may feel overwhelmed with sadness and grief. The feelings you have may not officially qualify as clinical depression, but sadness and grief may be emotions you experience for a while as you come to terms with The Law. The implications of its existence are huge. You may even consider blaming yourself for various "bad" experiences you had in the past.

Again, it is completely normal to go through a period of having those thoughts accompanied by sadness. But blame is not relevant here. Before you were aware of The Law, you didn't know that your thoughts caused your experiences. You were not aware of the rules of the game of life.

If you played soccer without knowing the rules, you may decide to kick the ball into your own goal, which would give the other team the point. Would you blame yourself for that if no one had taught you that the object of the game was to only kick the ball into your opponent's net? No, you wouldn't blame yourself.

In the same way, don't blame yourself for previous unpleasant experiences because you had no awareness of the rules of the game. Processing and getting through any feelings of sadness and depression is important. Doing so will help you better prepare to create the positive, successful experiences you desire in the future.

As we've already said, ignoring these emotions would take you into denial, which only slows down the process of acceptance and moving past your emotional baggage. If or when this stage comes, face it head on.

Acceptance

When you finally get to full acceptance of The Law, you are ready to experiment with it. You will understand that your experiments are no longer about either proving or disapproving the existence of The Law. Your experiments will now be about developing a deeper understanding of how The Law works and a proficiency in using it to create more of what you want.

If the emotions are very intense, physical movement can often be beneficial. Dancing, riding a bike, hiking, running, walking, punching a heavy bag, kickboxing, or whatever physical activity you enjoy can help you release any pent-up emotion. Being outside is always beneficial to lighten the burden of heavy emotion. As John Burroughs said, "I go to nature to be soothed and healed and have my senses put in tune once more."

For many people, massage can unlock emotions trapped in the cells. Just don't be surprised if you end up crying or feeling angry while on the massage table. It's a healthy way to release locked emotions and most massage and other hands-on therapists are quite accustomed to it happening.

If you have serious emotional wounding, get help from someone trained and knowledgeable in that area. Professional support will not only help you face the current situation, but can give you tools to better handle unexpected situations as they arise in the future.

Exercise:

Jot down any insights you've gained while reading this chapter.

As you contemplate the various stages of mourning, write how you are feeling in your journal. Expressing on paper any anger or sadness that surfaces is a great way to get your emotions "out" in a constructive, helpful way. Sometimes emotions just need acknowledgement and expression to release. Writing works as a great form of expression with no destructive ramifications. Always use pen on paper as it uses much more of the creative parts of the brain. As you write about the emotions you experience, you may remember situations and gain great insights.

Key Concepts

- Working with The Law is a journey with highs and lows.
- When first learning about The Law, a series of emotions can surface and must be dealt with.
- Once you accept that The Law is real, you can then begin to really utilize The Law to achieve your desires.

Baby Steps

While The Law has no limits, your belief about what is personally possible forms a limitation that must be overcome. The importance of belief is paramount in manifesting success, and we cover it in great detail later on.

It's important to distinguish that your belief about what is personally possible for you to manifest differs from your belief in The Law itself.

When first learning about The Law, many people get stars in their eyes and immediately decide they want a million dollars. But few actually believe that having a million dollars is something they can personally achieve. Programming The Law for something you don't believe is possible is a fast way to failure.

After the million dollars invariably fails to appear, people often jump to the conclusion that The Law isn't real and they give up trying to understand or work with it. Because failure often leads to giving up, we highly recommend that you start small.

On the off chance that someone managed to get the million dollars, most are not ready for it. Those lucky few who actually win the lottery (you're far more likely to get struck by lightning by the way) usually spend all of it, after taxes of course, within a few years. Even when they did achieve that wild dream, they weren't psychologically prepared or financially knowledgeable enough to handle it.

Another reason to start with small simple experiments is that if you start out too big, it's easy to get a lot of "noise" in your experimental results that make it difficult to draw obvious conclusions. "Noise" means too many factors or variables to easily determine which one had the greatest impact or played the biggest role in the success or failure of your experiment. Starting small ensures you can draw clear conclusions which will lead to having more successful experiments in the future.

A commonly recommended initial experiment is getting an ideal parking space to park your car in. There are several reasons it makes such a splendid choice:

1. It is far easier to believe that you can find an open parking space than to manifest something big like the million-dollar example we mentioned earlier.
2. Often when you really need a spot close to the main entrance of a location, you have a lot of passion and energy about finding it.
3. You probably can think of times in the past when you found a great parking space ... *even if you thought at the time that it was by luck or chance.* You know how great it felt when it happened and can use that as fuel for creating

an ideal parking space in your new experiment.

———◆———

Mark:

I didn't choose to manifest a parking space as one of my first experiments. I chose, instead, to manifest a luggage cart on the last day of my family vacation at the beach resort we visit often.

Resort guests use luggage carts to transport their luggage to and from their car to their condo. On this particular trip, my family's condo was on the fifth floor of a high-rise building. Without a luggage cart, it would've taken me many, many trips and a lot of physical exertion to get everything from the condo back to the car before heading home.

On the last day of our vacation, we were not the only family leaving and in need of a luggage cart. There were far more families in need of a cart than there were carts available. This led to many families hoarding carts. The resort always puts the carts out the day before leaving day. Almost immediately, people take the carts back to their rooms to be sure they had one the next day. Within a noticeably short time, there were no luggage carts to be found.

I used to be one of those people who grabbed a cart as soon as they appeared, fearing there would not be any the next day when I needed one. This time, I decided not to hoard a cart, but to use it as an experiment of manifesting one at precisely the time I needed it.

When the luggage carts appeared, my mother-in-law asked if we should get one. I said, "No. I am confident one will be available tomorrow when I need it." While I didn't tell her I was experimenting with The Law, she still looked at me like I was crazy for not taking a cart when I could.

As I walked through the lobby in the early morning on my way to enjoy the sunrise on the last day of our vacation, there were no carts. I knew that wasn't a problem because it wasn't yet time for us to leave.

For the next few hours, I went through the lobby several times as we enjoyed our last day at the beach. I never saw an available cart the whole day.

It was finally time to move our stuff out of the condo and into the car, so I headed toward the lobby. As I enter the elevator, I envisioned (imagined) a cart being available when I got there. As the elevator stopped and the doors opened, I looked out and saw no carts. I walked out of the elevator, turned right, and there it was. A lone luggage cart waiting just for me.

I was thrilled that my experiment had worked. It was one more piece of evidence pointing to The Law being real. I was moving closer and closer to full acceptance of The Law. I was even more excited to continue my pursuit of understanding how it works.

Exercise:

Jot down in your journal any insights you've gained while reading this chapter.

Try the experiment to get a great parking space. Revisit that section of the chapter and follow the steps. Journal about how the experiment went and what you learned from it.

Key Concepts

- When first working with The Law, it's important to do small experiments. They are easier and far more likely to succeed.
- The more success you have with The Law, the more your confidence will build.
- Confidence leads you to bigger wins with The Law.

The Big Picture

Before diving into the nitty-gritty details, we need to look at the bigger picture. We've developed an elegantly simple formula that explains how your thoughts become your reality. It helps you work with The Law in a way that is far easier to understand and use than anything else we've come across.

The Computer Analogy

Every thought you have is sending signals to the Universe about what you want. You'll learn later that whatever you send (positive or negative) is interpreted by the Law as something you want, even if that's not your intention. Every thought or mental signal is like typing on a keyboard into a computer. The computer is the Universe and the processing system (that does something with it) is The Law. As you think about various things, you send out a signal and The Law transforms it into your life experience.

A 3-D printer is a great example. 3-D printers take a string of material (often plastic), melt it, and deposit it in a structured sequence (based on a program). The result is a new physical object. That object can be anything the programmer can imagine (design and program).

Figure 2. 3D Printer

The 3-D printer needs a specific design (blueprint) programmed into its computer before it can create anything. Just like the computer design tells the 3-D printer what object to create, your mental programs (or signals) form the blueprints The Law needs to create your reality.

New Science of Success Formula™

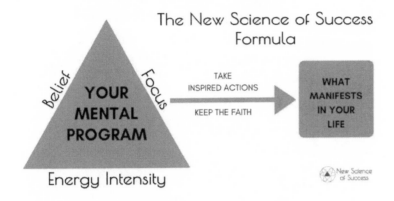

Figure 3. New Science of Success Formula

The above diagram shows the complete *New Science of Success Formula™*. It includes your *Mental Programming Triangle* (belief, focus, energy intensity) to signal the Universe exactly what you want followed by taking inspired actions and keeping the faith over time. The critical components of the Mental Programming Triangle (or Programming Triangle) are:

- **Belief** - You must believe (even sub-consciously) that owning the thing you want or having the experience you desire is personally possible for you. You can't manifest or experience anything that you don't actually believe you can. Belief trips up most people when trying to program The Law on purpose.

- **Focus** (Thought) - The Law responds to your thoughts that are most clearly formed and are most frequently on your mind when paired with the next factor. If you put jumbled, conflicting, rambling thoughts in, you will get jumbled, conflicting, rambling experiences out (in your reality and daily experience).

- **Energy Intensity -** The energy intensity behind your thought acts like an accelerator. The greater the energy intensity (positive or negative) you have about the thought, the more likely that thought is to manifest and the more quickly the manifestation is likely to occur. Fear, excitement, joy, absolute certainty all work as forms of powerful energy intensity.

Once the Mental Program is in place, there are two additional factors required to get what you want:

- **Inspired Action** - To achieve or receive the things you want, actions are most often required. Sometimes, many actions must take place. Inspired actions are those actions you feel prompted from within (through intuition) to take. Inspired actions have a far greater impact on achieving and/or receiving your desires than normal actions that you figured out through logic or took because some "expert" said you should take them. Normal actions are often based on experiences from the past. Taking normal actions often results in experiencing the same or similar results to those you always have.

- **Keep the Faith** (not giving up) - Maintaining a belief in The Law and not giving in to doubt is vital to your success. Once you've sent your Mental Program and begin taking inspired actions, if the thing you want to manifest doesn't show up quickly, it's easy to start believing (or fearing) it will never happen. When you begin to doubt The Law and your ability to have what you desire, you screw up the program and you'll never get the result you were aiming for. "Keep the faith" is about never doubting that The Law is real and working on your behalf, even if what you want doesn't show up as quickly as you might hope.

When you can master these five factors, you can manifest anything.

The Law never malfunctions. People, however, often malfunction as they attempt to control these five factors and improve their lives.

Exercise:

Jot down in your journal any insights you've gained while reading this chapter.

Think of something you've tried to manifest (a new job, a romantic partner, a trip to somewhere wonderful) or a change you've tried to make (lose 10 lbs, learn a new skill, stop biting your nails) and failed *(so far anyway)*.

Think about the five factors and consider the role they played in your lack of success at achieving that desire. Write about it in your journal.

Key Concepts

- You'll have more success if you understand the big picture first.
- The three critical factors to programming The Law are belief, focus, and energy intensity.
- The two additional factors necessary to bring your desires into reality are taking inspired actions and keeping the faith.

What I Learned At the Airport

You are a powerful creator. To experience more of what you want, you must become intentional in your programming. It requires much more effort at first as you move from randomly and unconsciously programming The Law, as you've always done, to consistently intentionally programming it. This extra effort at first is normal and won't be needed forever.

Entropy may be an unfamiliar word for you. It's a primary element of the fundamental laws of physics which govern how our universe works. *(Don't worry, we promise not to get so science-y here that you get lost.)*

The laws of thermodynamics are the foundation of our modern physics. The 1st Law of Thermodynamics states that "Energy can neither be created nor destroyed; energy can only be transformed or changed from one form to another." Everything in the universe is energy, and that includes solid objects.

You've probably come across this 1st law before. But the second law may be one you are less familiar with.

The Second Law of Thermodynamics (the Law of Entropy) is continuously working against change. Your life is a system, and entropy is the level of disorder it contains. All systems prefer being in a highly disordered state as it takes less energy (effort) to maintain the disorder. So, even your life prefers to be in a state of disorder. Simply put, you prefer life to be as easy as possible.

While you may not have heard of entropy or the 2nd Law of Thermodynamics, we know you've experienced it many times in your life.

The Status Quo

You probably know the Law of Entropy by its more common name, the "status quo." That is the comfortable, familiar state of being where you operate on auto-pilot, going through life following old familiar patterns, thinking old familiar thoughts, and experiencing much of the same things day after day, week after week, year after year. You probably drive the same route to work each day, eat the same small selection of foods for lunch, and entertain the same thoughts and feelings about life all the time.

The status quo is an obvious example of the Law of Entropy. You probably "live there" most of the time.

Remember that this law states that a system prefers to be in its lowest energy state. The status quo is your lowest energy state. And we all like to stay there. It's far easier to live in entropy. You don't need to put much effort into what you are thinking, saying, doing, or feeling to remain happily in the status quo. You just repeat past patterns again and again, which inevitably lead to exactly the same or similar results.

If you are attempting to manifest something new and you haven't realized that a great deal of effort is needed to make the change happen, then you're probably experiencing what Einstein calls insanity. He said, "Insanity is doing the same thing over and over and expecting different results." Anyone wanting their life to change, but continuing to think, say, do, and feel the same things they always have are highly unlikely to achieve that desired change.

It takes a lot of effort. Most people need a catalyst (some big incentive) to put the necessary effort in to make a change. Two highly effective incentives are:

- a pain or situation they can no longer endure
- a desire so compelling they will do whatever it takes to achieve it

As you try to make changes, you have a fundamental law of physics working against you and the desires you have for new experiences and levels of success. It's a worthwhile challenge to overcome.

The Lego Analogy

A simple way to understand entropy or the energy state of a system is by observing Lego building blocks. It takes little energy to dump the Legos out of a container onto the floor. Kids have no problem dumping out the Legos. It's easy. It takes mere seconds. The lowest energy state for the Legos is being scattered everywhere.

But if you've ever built a building or some other structure with Legos, you know it takes much more time and effort than it did to scatter them onto the floor. Placing the Legos one by one into the structure of a building organizes them and puts them into a state of order. This is a much higher energy state than being scattered all over the place.

Even if you built nothing with the scattered Legos, you know it takes far more effort and time to put them back into their container than it did to dump them out. That's why it's difficult getting children to put away their Legos or other toys when they're finished playing.

Think of manifesting new experiences through The Law like building with Legos. The Law has all the stuff it needs to create the experiences you want to build. The stuff is like the Legos. But The Law can only build what you let it know you want it to build.

You are always broadcasting your desires to The Law because you're always thinking. We go into detail about how that works later. It takes energy and effort to focus your thoughts toward the experiences you desire. It's easier to just allow your thoughts to come and go as they do. This is entropy at work. To move from random signals to intentional signals being sent requires activation energy (effort) on your part.

The key to subduing entropy is realizing that it takes effort to move from where you are right now to where you want to be. You have to move out of your comfortable, auto-pilot way of life into a more deliberate, focused way of being. It requires effort to intentionally aim your focus on what you desire most.

———◆———

The Airport Analogy

Mark:

I think of entropy and activation energy every time I'm at an airport. Before it's time to board the plane, passengers are scattered about the terminal shopping, eating, drinking, relaxing, or doing anything to help pass the time before their flight. There is little energy required to scatter the passengers throughout the airport. It's easy ... *much like dumping the Legos.*

When it's time to board, however, that disordered state of scattered passengers, easily moving about the airport must transform. They need to organize into a single line so everyone can board the plane.

I can feel the activation energy going on each time I go through this boarding process.

Gate agents are herding passengers into a line to pass the single point to scan boarding passes. People are no longer free and happy. They become agitated and competitive, jockeying to get on the plane before others. The process is slow as the line forms, people walk down the jetway, board the plane, find their seats, stow their carry-on baggage, take off their jacket, and ask the person in the aisle to stand so they can take the middle or window seat. There is a lot of activation energy required to seat each individual passenger into the well-ordered seat configuration of the aircraft. A plane of seated passengers is definitely not in the lowest energy state.

The flight takes off and eventually reaches its ultimate destination. Again you witness the 2nd Law of Thermodynamics in action. You feel the release of the energy and the relief of the passengers as they break free from the high energy, low entropy, highly ordered state of being bottled up in individual seats on the plane. The passengers flow out at seemingly lightning speed and quickly disperse into the crowd of other passengers in the airport terminal. They are now again in a lower energy state, freely flowing from the arrival gate to their next departing gate or baggage claim.

———◆———

Think about the thoughts randomly floating around your head like the passengers milling about waiting for the boarding time of a flight. To manifest, you have to purposefully input activation energy (working hard to pay attention) to weed out the thoughts of things you don't want while shifting your focus onto things you do want. And you have to keep it up long enough so this new state of focus and intention becomes your new normal (status quo). We'll teach you ways to do that in upcoming chapters.

Entropy is a universal law that drives everything to remain the same. But with effort and persistence, you can create a new status quo, a new state of focused thought that becomes your new lowest energy state ... your new normal. This new state of easy focused thought leads to the new experiences you desire.

The Spaceship Analogy

A spaceship is a great analogy to illustrate this idea. For a spaceship to take off from the surface of the earth, it takes an incredible amount of energy. Think about the fiery rocket propulsion that you've seen on TV when a satellite launches into orbit. It takes an extreme amount of energy to propel it into space. But once it's up at its desired distance from earth, the energy required to remain in orbit is much less.

Figure 4. Spaceship

Your personal journey with The Law is about moving your life into a new orbit ... one of greater success, happiness, and fulfillment. You need an enormous boost of extra energy (effort) to get out of status quo and into that new orbit or way of life. Once there, less energy and effort are needed to maintain that orbit or level of success.

It's like climbing a steep section on the mountain. It's physically quite hard. You have to carefully take each step. But then it levels out and you walk on flat ground for a while before it's time to climb again ... *to your next level of success.*

———◆———

Takara

Tenacity could be my middle name. And to get over entropy, I suggest you become pretty tenacious yourself. Not giving up, being willing to do whatever it takes to achieve your dreams, that has often been my motto.

I put myself through college. I worked full time during the day, went to school full time in the evenings, and was engaged. I have a vivid memory of sitting on my bed one morning and suddenly laughing out loud at how absurd the situation seemed. In front of me was a book and notes that I was studying for class. In one hand was the hairdryer I was using to dry my hair. In my other hand was the fork I was using to eat breakfast. To accomplish all I needed to, I had to become a multitasking ninja. When people give up because they find things a bit difficult, me sitting on the bed doing three things at once always comes to mind. That's what I'm willing to do to get things done. Stay up late. Get up early. Multi-task. Work hard when necessary. Rest when I can. Then get up and do it again.

Contrast that with my fiancé's behavior … *the guy I mentioned on my first vision board.* He let entropy stop him from going after his greatest dream in life. It's one of several reasons I broke off our engagement.

He wanted to be a Forest Ranger. His family had recently moved from downtown Detroit to the beautiful Blue Ridge Mountains. He discovered a love for camping and fishing, and spent hours in the woods with his dog. Being in nature was his "happy place." Forest Ranger was the perfect job for him. Yet, when he discovered that Calculus was required to get a forestry degree, he refused to even try.

I was pretty astonished by that decision. The only thing standing between him and his greatest career dream was one freaking class. One class. But rather than think, "I'll just have to do whatever it takes, get a tutor, take the class twice, whatever, to pass that class," he simply gave up the dream … didn't even sign up for a forestry degree. It made me wonder, "If I stay with this guy, how many things are we going to not do, not achieve, not have because there is some effort involved?" The "giving up because it's hard" mindset just didn't work for me. And, as I mentioned, several additional factors went into the decision that it was time to part ways.

I learned years later that he did finally get that forestry degree. It made me smile, knowing he finally went after and achieved that dream.

It's useful to have a plan and a roadmap to help you feel more confident that this burst of activation energy (effort) to a new life is worth it. Our systematic approach offers just such a roadmap for you. It's time to dive into the details so you can begin manifesting on purpose.

Exercise:

Jot down in your journal any insights you've gained while reading this chapter.

Reflect on times when you pushed yourself and were able to achieve something. Write about how it made you feel.

Think about times when you've wanted something, but because it seemed too hard or it didn't show up in your life as fast as you'd hoped, you gave up on that dream. Write about that in your journal.

Key Concepts

- It is far easier to continue doing things the way you have always done them. However, that means your life will continue the way it is now without achieving the dreams you desire.
- Change requires effort.
- In the beginning, it takes a great deal of effort.

What Do You Believe?

We all have limitless potential. However, what you achieve and experience is largely based on what you believe is actually possible. Belief, therefore, is one of the three critical factors in the Mental Programming Triangle used to tell the Universe which experiences you most want.

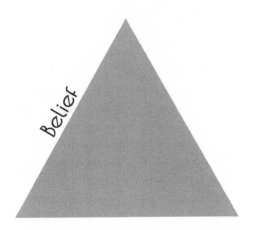

Figure 5. Belief

The tricky part about looking at, and understanding, beliefs is that what you believe consciously is often in conflict with what you believe subconsciously. Many of the beliefs you have about yourself and how life works formed so long ago you may be unaware that some of them are even part of your belief system.

How Beliefs Form:

The beliefs you hold, whether positive or negative, come from several sources. Some come from the people you surround yourself with. Others come from experiences you've had that caused you to draw conclusions about how life works. Some you get through your DNA. Studies have shown that phobias can be passed down for 14 generations.[25] Empathic people can take on the beliefs of others without even knowing it. Dr. Judith Orloff says empaths are those who absorb the world's joys and stresses like "emotional sponges."[26]

With so many avenues to pick up negative beliefs, it's almost impossible not to have at least a few.

Some people that influence your beliefs:

- parents
- teachers
- ministers/rabbis/priests
- coaches
- friends
- family
- bosses
- colleagues
- bullies

- others you encounter.

You are, right now, the sum total of your previous experiences beginning at conception. In the early years before starting school, your parents influenced your worldview along with how you first thought about yourself:

- who you are
- if you are a good or bad person
- if you are talented, smart, or doomed to failure

Through your school years, you had additional influences from teachers, friends (and enemies), coaches, ministers (rabbis, priests, etc.), and youth leaders that significantly contributed to what you think about yourself even to this day.

Maybe there was a teacher who told you that you weren't smart enough or a coach who said you were not good enough for the sport or activity you loved. Perhaps a parent said you were a disappointment, constantly compared you to a sibling or friend, or that you needed to become a doctor and not the artist, dancer, or musician you wanted in your heart to become.

Mark:

I remember being told from a very young age that "money goes where money is." My family was not the place where money was, so I logically concluded that money would not be flowing my way ... *ever.*

This thought about money was not my belief, but I allowed it to become my belief based on what I heard from my parents. After almost half a century, I finally replaced that old view of money that was hacked into my beliefs from others with beliefs about money that I chose. I now know that money goes to where thoughts about money and beliefs about money are. "As I think, so shall I experience" is my new money mantra.

———————◆———————

Takara:

I have a very distinct memory of an imprint I received from my parents about how life and money works. I was in grade school and my best friend's parents had taken the entire family to Club Med in the Caribbean somewhere. We lived in Texas and spent most summer days lounging and playing at the country club pool. But my friend came back with an even better tan than she already had. She told me stories of white sandy beaches, palm trees, and turquoise seas. She even brought me back gifts, including a poster of the beach where she'd had her vacation. Anyone who knows me knows how deeply connected I am to the ocean. Seeing the beach and hearing fabulous stories about being there made me long for that experience. And it made me wonder why my family never took vacations like that.

So, I asked my parents about it. "Why is it that Kathy's parents put the whole family on a plane and go to places like Club Med on vacation while we always drive for days in a car, stay at Holiday Inns and eat at Stuckey's on vacation?"

I'll never forget my father's response: "There are two kinds of people in this world. There are savers and there are squanderers. In the end, those who save have lots of money, and those who squander money end up with nothing." Well, there was no question about which category my family fit into. We never squandered even a penny. I felt deeply deflated and had a sick feeling in my stomach, thinking that I'd never have the things I want in life. It felt like a sentence worse than death.

Thank heavens during college I made that vision board and proved to myself that I could have the things I truly want. Some strongly imprinted beliefs take a lot of work to overcome, and that belief is one I wrestled with repeatedly over the years.

———◆———

Negativity Can Affect Your Program:

It is very difficult to not take in and believe what you are told by others ... *particularly if you view them as authority figures.* The people you surround yourself with continually share their opinions, beliefs, and fears about various things. A few examples (negative beliefs you may have heard are in parentheses):

- how life works (if you work night and day you will eventually be successful, things never work out, relationships are hard)
- how "those people" are (rich people are all ___, bosses are all ___, men are all ___, women are all ___)
- how money works (the root of all evil, doesn't grow on trees, better not squander all of it, better save for a rainy day, that's too expensive, we could never afford that)
- what is best for you (you should do this, you should do that, better not date that one because ___, better not move there because ___, better not be friends with that person because ___, that job is terrible because ___, better avoid ___ because ___, if you don't do ___ there will be hell to pay)
- what you are not good at (women are terrible at math, you are too clumsy to be a dancer, you

are too stupid or lazy, etc. to be ___ or to have
___)
- what career options are likely for people like us
(poor, a woman, people of various ethnicities or
religions, various physical or mental handicaps,
someone who didn't go to college, etc.)

Making these fears and limitations a part of your
belief system is much like having a virus in your
computer. These negative belief "viruses" must be
eradicated or the Programs you broadcast will be faulty.
They create a boundary on what you can experience.

Exercise:
Jot down in your journal any insights you've gained
while reading this chapter.

Think about your limiting beliefs and try to identify
when and how they began. Write about it in your journal.

Key Concepts

- We all have limiting beliefs of one kind or another.
- Limiting beliefs place boundaries on what can be created through The Law.
- Limiting beliefs must be released in order to manifest the things you desire.

Signaling the Universe

While all three factors (belief, focus, and energy intensity) are needed to manifest an experience into reality, belief sets the stage for what you focus on.

We often show the three Mental Programming factors as the sides of a triangle.

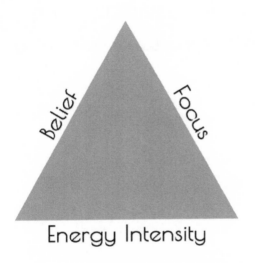

Figure 6. Mental Programming Triangle

The Fire Triangle Analogy

The fire triangle is a good analogy for understanding how the three Mental Programming factors work together.

Making a fire requires oxygen, fuel (wood), and a spark (match). If you get a nice load of firewood prepared and you don't have a match or some other way to create heat like a spark, you'll never have a fire.

Figure 7. Fire Triangle

Your belief in what is personally possible is like the oxygen required for a campfire. You could get excited as you focus on something you really want, but if that desire is something you don't believe is actually possible for you personally to experience, it won't happen.

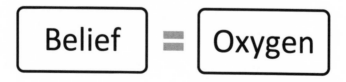

Actually, it is very difficult to even hold a focus for long on an experience you don't believe is possible. You may think about the experience for a moment. But your limiting beliefs will take over and snuff out any possibility of that thought ever becoming your actual life experience.

Limiting beliefs don't have to be permanent. You can overcome them and expand into new potentials.

In fact, the discovery and dissolution of disempowering beliefs can be one of the greatest challenges and most powerful rewards of personal growth, learning how to manifest, and achieving greater and greater success.

Using various tools, methods, and techniques, you can uncover your limiting beliefs and free yourself from the powerful grip they've had. When that happens, possibilities open up and your life begins to change ... *sometimes dramatically*. We offer some ways to address limiting beliefs in later chapters.

These are necessary steps that everyone has to take to go from wherever they are currently in their career, with their finances, or relationships, to where they want to be.

As you release these fears and limitations, you are expanding your belief boundary in a way that allows you to have and experience more of what you desire and less of what you don't.

Exercise:

Jot down in your journal any insights you've gained while reading this chapter.

Start a new page in your journal and create a two-column list. Simply draw a line down the center of the page from top to bottom.

At the top of the column on the left, write: " Things I believe I can have, do, or become." At the top of the column on the right, write: "Things I don't believe I can have, do, or become."

Think of all the things you desire and write them underneath the appropriate heading creating a list of things you do believe are possible on the left and those you don't believe are possible on the right.

Remember, baby steps. Because the things on the left are already believable, those are great things to experiment with manifesting first.

As you have more and more success, come back to this page in your journal and see if you can move any of the items on the right over to the left. The more success you have, the more you believe is possible. Perhaps one day, there will be nothing whatsoever on the right-hand side.

Key Concepts

- You can't manifest or experience what you don't believe is personally possible for you.
- Your beliefs around what is personally possible are as important to manifesting as oxygen is for a fire.
- Belief is the foundation for everything you experience in life.

Influencing & Being Influenced

Mark:

I discovered, as I suspect you may have also, if you've tried previously to manifest with LOA, it's not as easy as some make it seem. After I read *Think and Grow Rich* by Napoleon Hill, I tried to follow the recommendations in the book. But I found it somewhat confusing. Giving it my best was met with limited success.

Hill's book focused primarily on creating financial success, as many books about LOA do. So, I decided I should choose a dollar figure and set a target date for manifesting it. I struggled to figure out an amount. I thought about choosing $1 million. But I immediately figured out that I didn't really believe that was possible ... *not in the beginning, anyway.*

As I look back, I realize I also had little energy or excitement around manifesting a million dollars. The idea of creating any specific financial number didn't inspire me. I did eventually come up with something that was less than a million, in a range that I could half-heartedly say I believed. Deep down, though, I knew I didn't even believe that number was possible.

It should come as no surprise that when the date I wrote for achieving my financial goal came, I was in the same place, with the same job, making the same salary. My financial goal didn't happen.

I could've easily taken this apparent failure and ended my pursuit of understanding The Law right there. Fortunately, however, I intuitively sensed that The Law was real and kept going. I concluded that I just didn't know enough about how it worked yet.

Using my training and experience as a scientist seemed the best way to find the keys needed to unlock how The Law works.

A new opportunity to experiment presented itself. My seven-year-old daughter had just finished her second year on a summer swim team and qualified to take part in the league championship. She was very proud of that accomplishment and decided she wanted to join a winter team. Winter swimming is more competitive and participants are more committed to the sport.

Very early in the season, her coach asked each swimmer to write down their goals. She and I discussed the goals she was considering. She said she wanted to qualify for the All-Star meet.

Being a numbers guy, I looked at the qualifying times for that event from previous years. Her times weren't yet fast enough to achieve that goal. I felt if she worked really hard and got significantly faster, she might qualify.

The easiest choice would have been to suggest that maybe she should spend this first year of winter swimming, having fun and learning more so she could continue improving. Maybe making the All-Star meet could be a goal better saved for the following season. After all, she was only seven and this was her first year as a serious competitive swimmer. A responsible, loving parent would surely try to protect her from feeling bad by not achieving what was clearly an unrealistic goal.

As we talked, I thought about The Law. "Think, believe, receive," became "think, believe, achieve" in my mind. So, I chose not to advise her to set a lesser goal than the one she had decided on. I instead told her that I believed she could qualify for the All-Star meet. I didn't feel that I was filling her with false hope. At that moment, I really believed it was possible ... *unlike my previous personal experiment with the large financial goal.* My belief helped her believe it as well.

As the season progressed, she was making improvements in her backstroke but wasn't yet at the level she needed to qualify for the All-Star meet. Her times in the other strokes weren't even close. The butterfly, for example, was a stroke she only swam for the first time in competition the previous summer. All the parents applauded her for the effort as she barely made it across the pool. She was working hard at practice and even her butterfly was improving. But making the All-Star meet in any stroke was looking more and more unlikely.

On a wintry Saturday morning in January, her team attended a meet aptly named the Frosty Frolic. One event she was competing in was the 100 Individual Medley (IM). In the IM, each swimmer swims 25 yards of each of the four swim strokes. She had not swum this event much but you can't get better at something without working on it.

It came time for her heat. She dove off the starting block to begin the first 25-yard leg swimming the butterfly. As I watched her swim down the lane, I looked over at my wife and asked, "who is that in her lane?" She was swimming a fantastic butterfly. Suddenly, this girl who could barely make it across the pool was now looking like a future Olympian. It was a delightful surprise.

She continued to improve. Her times in both the butterfly and backstroke moved her into the All-Star range. When the selections came in, she qualified in both events. That was amazing. The butterfly was not even on the radar at the start of the season. She believed she could do it, and she did. She was so proud of her accomplishments.

These initial experiments with The Law showed that a belief in what is personally possible is vital to successfully manifesting with The Law.

The experiment with my daughter highlighted one other important thing about belief. You're not only responsible for developing your own belief, but you can also influence the beliefs of those close to you, especially your children. Everything you say to your children, your spouse, your friends, your family, your students, your athletes, your colleagues, your direct reports, or anyone you closely interact with has the power to influence the beliefs of that person.

Conversely, the beliefs of those around you can have a significant influence on what you believe is possible. If you surround yourself with people who think you can achieve what you want, you're far more likely to succeed. Whereas if you surround yourself with people who constantly belittle you and say it's impossible, you're far more likely to accept that as truth and give up before you even get started.

----◆----

You need to ask yourself if you are helping or hindering the personal beliefs of others. Are you squashing their dreams by replacing them with something you think is more likely, or probable? You may feel that you're helping your child set realistic goals with the well-intentioned notion that you're protecting them from some future heartache because of failure. Such an approach serves only to pass along your limiting beliefs to them.

Sara Blakely, the founder of Spanx, the woman's undergarment company, understood the potentially powerful influence of others. In an interview in Success, Blakely shared how she kept her idea for Spanx a secret from her family and friends for a full year until the business was ready to launch.[27] She knew that her well-meaning family and friends would likely tell her all the ways her business idea would fail to protect her from disappointment.

Blakely's business idea went into the stratosphere. Her net worth is now in the billion-dollar range. Her story shows the potential of The Law when you're highly focused and you believe the success you want is truly possible for you to experience.

The beliefs of those around you can have a significant influence on what you believe. If you surround yourself with people who think you can achieve what you want, you're far more likely to do it. Whereas if you're surrounded by people who constantly belittle you and say it's impossible, you're far more likely to accept that as truth and give up before you even get started.

Have you ever been so aware of how the beliefs of others could sabotage yours that you kept your goals a secret? We both discovered that we have greater success with The Law when we keep our dreams and goals to ourselves.

Of course, when the goal you are setting involves another, then everyone involved should participate in setting that goal. When we are making plans for the New Science of Success, this book, and the various programs we are developing, we do that together by phone or video chat. The same is true for the collaborations we each have with others. People have far more energy and enthusiasm about something when they take part in setting the initial dream or vision for it together.

Belief in what is personally possible is the foundation to manifesting through The Universal Law of Creation. Your belief affects the other two critical components. It's difficult to focus on, and bring to fruition, an idea or desire if you don't actually believe that it's something you could ever experience. It's equally difficult to become highly energized or excited by such ideas.

Increasing your belief isn't as simple as turning on a light switch. Going from no belief to believing that absolutely anything is possible doesn't happen in one swift move. Instead of trying to take a gigantic leap in what you believe to be possible, the expansion of your beliefs can best occur by creating a series of wins that are smaller in scope, but that you can actually believe are possible for you.

You live in a world that has learned to expect instant gratification. It's a world of convenience where almost anything you want or need is available in minutes, hours, or days. Entire wars are waged and won in a two-hour movie.

If you try to achieve goals using The Law with an instant gratification mindset, you are almost guaranteed to be disappointed. You are likely to fall into that 90% of people who say they have little to no success with LOA.[28] And you also risk erroneously concluding that The Universal Law of Creation is a bunch of hooey.

As we move on to Focus, the next critical component in the Programming Triangle, keep the concept of small wins in mind as you consider what goal to focus on manifesting. Try not to go so big that you don't really believe the experience is possible.

On the flip side, try not to focus on something so close to your current experience that you aren't able to tell if The Law was really at play when you manifest it. As you experiment with The Law, stretch yourself a little beyond your comfort zone with something you want to manifest that has been just out of reach.

Exercise:

Jot down in your journal any insights you've gained while reading this chapter.

Write in your journal about times you can remember when someone influenced your personal beliefs.

Also, think and write about times when you influenced the beliefs of another. Your children perhaps?

Key Concepts

- Your personal beliefs are easily influenced by those closest to you.
- You are also influencing the beliefs of others including your spouse or partner, children, friends, students, even your boss.
- Minimizing or eliminating altogether the negative belief influences of others is a key to manifesting greater success.

What's Hiding in Plain Sight?

To experience more of what you want, you often have to grow and develop as an individual ... *sometimes in significant ways*. That always involves addressing issues, beliefs, fears, and more that hold you back. As we've mentioned before, you may not even be consciously aware of some limiting beliefs you have.

Don't worry.

We all have them.

And the job of finding them and eradicating them is never complete. It's just a peeling away of layers and layers of falsehood ... *like layers of an onion*.

The 9 Veils of Illusion™

Every truly worthwhile and life-changing self-help or success course addresses these things.

Takara:

Having read a little of my history, you know I had quite a few issues to address. I got help from professionals, read a lot of books, took numerous classes and workshops, and even developed several methods myself for overcoming things from my past. I kept looking at the issues I faced and that of my clients and had this powerful inner knowing that there had to be a finite list of things that kept us (humanity) from happiness and success.

One day I simply asked The Universe (God by whatever name you prefer) for the list. A few days later, I woke up with this list fully formed, simply waiting for me to write it down. I call these nine issues, *The 9 Veils of Illusion*™ or the 9 Deadly Sins. They are what we all need to address to experience happiness, transform our lives, and achieve sustained success.

The 9 Veils of Illusion™ are:

1. Fear
2. Limiting Beliefs
3. Judgments
4. Expectations
5. Attachments to Outcomes
6. Guilt
7. Shame
8. Blame
9. Victimhood

Fear: Everyone is afraid of something. Some of these fears include heights, spiders, or that we will fail. Fear keeps you firmly stuck in mediocrity.

Most of us run these core human fears to varying degrees:

- being unworthy
- being unlovable
- being abandoned or rejected
- death

Many people are even more afraid of public speaking than they are of death. People don't like to speak publically because they're afraid of rejection and ridicule (which subconsciously means the tribe might abandon us). In our cave dweller days, tribal rejection meant fending for yourself in the wilderness, risking encounters with saber-tooth tigers or starvation. Sadly, we have these basic survival fears still running our lives.

Limiting Beliefs: The beliefs that keep you from going after your dreams and achieving your highest potential. Some of these include beliefs about how life is, how you are, how other people are, and about the Divine (God by all the various names).

Thoughts like, "I'm not smart enough," "I'm not pretty enough," "I should have gone to college," etc. will stop you every time. We shared several of these in the chapter on belief.

Judgments: We hold judgments toward ourselves and others and they are a huge hindrance to our success. Humans tend to judge situations, people, and things as right or wrong, good or bad.

Discernment is one thing. Judgment is something else entirely. Discernment comes without emotion. It happens through observation and reaching conclusions based on facts. Judgment always has an emotion attached. Often severe judgments are based on fears or limiting beliefs. Judging all people of a certain race, job title, or religion as being a certain way comes from that place. Many people spend so much of their day judging the behavior of others as right or wrong, good or bad, they forget to live their own life. Many judge themselves even more harshly than others.

Expectations: That means having a firm opinion about how people are to behave, including yourself, and how situations are "supposed" to be. They often get upset when people don't behave the way they expect them to or situations don't go as they expected. Just like judgments, often the most severe expectations are toward self.

Attachments to Outcomes: Being attached to an outcome means having a specific desire and thinking things need to happen a certain way. The more regimented you are in the way you feel every day "must" be, the more upset you become when it isn't. People not showing up on time, cars breaking down, computers malfunctioning just mean it's time to head in a new direction and flow with the moment. Learn to let it go and be fully in the now without letting it ruin your entire day.

Guilt: It means feeling terrible about what you "should" have done or should not have done. Or things you should do. When you take actions out of guilt rather than love, there is no joy or sense of fulfillment. There is only a sense of obligation and often resentment. Guilt serves no one ever!

Shame: It means having a deep sense of being a bad person, as if you have done something terribly wrong. Most rape victims feel ashamed of the experience (even though it was completely beyond their control).

Blame: When you point fingers at others and believe they are the reason for your unhappiness and other negative life circumstances. Shit happens (pardon the language). People behave certain ways, situations unfold in a certain way, and people get their feelings or body hurt. Holding on to your anger or sadness about such events only keeps you stuck and does nothing to the other person. Saint Augustine said, "Resentment is like drinking poison and waiting for the other person to die."

Victimhood: This one goes hand in hand with blame. It means never taking responsibility for your part in an unpleasant situation that occurred. You can't step into your empowerment, reach your potential, or your dreams if you continue to consider yourself a victim and play the "poor me" card all the time. Staying stuck in victimhood is a sure way to create more situations where victimization occurs. It becomes a self-fulfilling prophecy.

How to Discover Your Hidden Beliefs:

The easiest way to identify limiting beliefs, fears, etc. is to notice when you get really angry, sad, or upset. These negative beliefs often show up during times of powerful emotion.

When you notice that you're upset, it's the perfect time to discover what hidden belief is "flaring." Often it has to do with experiences you've had in the past or how you believe people "should" behave or treat you.

There are many other ways to discover hidden beliefs.

A very simple way is to utilize an oracle deck as a daily or weekly practice or when you want to manifest something and it's not happening. Oracle card decks often help you form a bridge between the conscious mind and the subconscious mind.

Famous author, Colette Baron Reid, has created several psychology-based card decks to help you uncover the fears and limiting beliefs you hold. Wisdom of the Hidden Realms helps you uncover what some call the "shadow" or hidden beliefs.

Three of her other decks include cards and ways to read the cards that reveal things you may not know about yourself, but that can stop you from the success you desire. Those three are The Enchanted Map, Wisdom of the Oracle, and Oracle of the 7 Energies. It's best to read the accompanying guidebooks for instructions on how to best use an oracle deck. However, a simple way is to ask, "What do I need to know about ____?" as you shuffle the cards. Fill in the blank with whatever you are trying to manifest or focus on, such as my relationship, my health, my finances, this situation.

Some people use tarot cards similarly even using the same questioning technique. Unlike oracle cards where every deck is unique with each card having a unique meaning, Tarot is a fixed system where each card has a fixed meaning. You can interpret the cards intuitively, but the overall meaning a specific card has is the same across decks.

Once you have pulled a card, write about it in your journal. As you contemplate the card and the given meaning, you will often have flashes of insight. Be sure to capture those in your journal. You may remember situations and moments that you had long forgotten. Most of the decks offer insights and information to shift your thinking in a more positive direction.

Contemplation for many people includes prayer and/or meditation, where you ask higher wisdom to give you insight into what the card is trying to show you.

You can do a contemplation exercise without using cards. Simply close your eyes and ask Divine wisdom to help you discover the blocks and limitations you are holding or believing that are keeping you stuck. Capture your thoughts in your journal.

Dissolution of The Veils:

When you notice yourself deeply upset, stop everything (if possible) and work to find out why. Ask yourself, "Why am I upset?" Journaling in moments like this can be enormously helpful. You begin by writing about the situation and then describe how angry or sad it made you feel.

Then ask yourself why it made you feel angry or sad.

Ask yourself if there was a previous time in your life when you felt that same way.

Takara suggests that there are "packets of emotion" that come when a particular limiting belief or fear is "running" (like a program in your subconscious mind). The same specific set of emotions comes as a package together whenever a specific subconscious negative belief is present. An example might be that something happens and you suddenly feel disrespected, sad, like you are being discounted. That is a "packet of emotion."

By journaling and looking back throughout your life for times when you felt that same set of emotions previously, you can often uncover the root cause of the limiting belief.

Write in your journal about that previous event.

Writing about it, acknowledging it, and realizing that it is crippling your happiness and ability to manifest, can sometimes be enough to release it and let it go.

Sometimes doing something physical besides the mental acknowledgment of it can be highly beneficial. You can pretend that you are gathering up this negative belief like a ball in your hands and then ceremoniously throw it away.

Some like to write the limiting belief on a piece of paper and burn it up (safely of course) in a candle, fireplace, or bowl designed for that purpose to ceremoniously let it go.

---◆---

Takara:

Many traditions use burning and releasing rituals. I lived in Santa Fe, NM for about 10 years and they have a tradition called Zozobra. They build a giant creature for the sole purpose of being publically burned. Those attending put all their unhappiness, the unpleasant things that have happened to them, etc. into Zozobra (through intention). Then this "monster" becomes a giant bonfire. From Wikipedia, "Zozobra is a 50 feet high giant marionette effigy that is built and burned during the annual Fiestas de Santa Fe in Santa Fe, New Mexico and marks the Fiestas' start. As his name suggests, he embodies gloom; by burning him, people destroy the worries and troubles of the previous year in the flames."[29]

---◆---

Screaming is another physical way preferred by some. While intending the release of the limitation, they make intense sounds with their voice. Other people can misinterpret screaming as a cry for help, so do it somewhere by yourself or let those who might hear you know what you are doing ahead of time. Screaming is not our preferred method. We included it here to give you more options to explore to find what works best for you.

Some people like to run, punch a heavy bag, dance, or do some other physical activity while focusing on releasing the negative belief or fear. Imagine negative thoughts and beliefs as small gray clouds or dark, icky blobs and as you walk, run, or dance, see them falling to the ground and being left behind.

It is best if you only address the issue that is "up" (causing emotional unrest) at the moment or the one you uncovered using an oracle or tarot deck rather than trying to release all your fears and limiting beliefs at once. Trying to release everything at once is often ineffective.

Try these various methods and begin addressing your 9 Veils of Illusion™. You will find releasing methods that resonate with you and seem to work better than others.

Much like the layers of an onion, deep-rooted issues often come back again and again at deeper levels. Do what you can to address them yourself, and if something refused to budge, it's time to get help.

There are endless forms of assistance available designed to help you release limiting beliefs trapped in the subconscious mind. A few include psychotherapy, shamanic journey, energy healing, hypnotherapy, rebirthing, Tapping, flower remedies, NLP, and many more. Takara often works 1-on-1 with private clients, helping them move beyond the 9 Veils using tools and techniques she developed.

Exercise:

Jot down in your journal any insights you've gained while reading this chapter.

Look back over the 9 Veils of Illusion™ in this chapter and write in your journal about any you feel may be negatively affecting you.

Can you pinpoint the events, or moments when these veils were first planted in your mind? Write about it in your journal.

Key Concepts

- There are 9 key things that keep you from experiencing greater happiness and success. We call these the 9 Veils of IllusionTM.
- It's important to identify which Veils impact you the most. Often, knowing when and how they became part of your belief system is helpful in eliminating them.
- Releasing the Veils is critical to strengthening your foundation of personal belief.

Focus is Key

The Universal Law of Creation is precise and consistent. It responds precisely to the Mental Programs or Signals you send. As mentioned previously, your Programs come from your belief (in what's possible for you), focus, and energy intensity (we cover that later on).

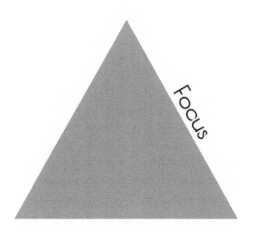

Figure 8. Focus

Your ability to have a crystal clear focus on what you want is like the fuel (firewood) needed to create a fire in the fire triangle diagram.

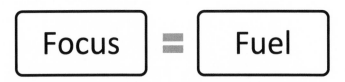

The Restaurant Analogy

The focus side of the Programming Triangle is like ordering from a menu. If you don't examine the menu options and make a definite choice, then you can't expect your waiter or waitress to know what you want. Without a firm decision, you could get absolutely anything on the menu ... *things you want and things you don't.*

The Law is like your waiter or waitress. It's constantly paying attention to the orders you place by your words, thoughts, and actions. You can't manifest (on purpose) the experiences you want to have until you first decide what it is that you truly want. And as we covered in the previous section, you need to believe that experience is personally possible as well.

Unlike the waiter or waitress who only handles your requests when you visit the restaurant, The Law is constantly receiving orders from you as you blast it with your thoughts ... *each one a new "order" indicating what you want.*

Researchers estimate that you have thousands of thoughts each day.[14] When you dump 50,000+ thoughts into the universe, it's unrealistic to expect The Law to deliver the one thing you really want amongst the tens of thousands of other potential experiences that you're broadcasting ... *unless you make it extremely clear.*

If you could hold a single consistent thought, The Law would know precisely which "order" to fill. Since such a level of focus is just about impossible for most people to maintain, The Law will work with the thoughts you have most often, that you believe are possible, and that you energize with the greatest intensity.

Negative Thoughts Often Hold Center Stage

Once you dig into your thoughts, really paying attention to them, you may find that your predominant thoughts, those with the greatest energy intensity and strongest belief, are about experiences you don't really want to have.

For example, frequently worrying about losing your job and fearing that losing your job is likely will often lead to you losing your job. Perhaps it's not losing your job that you worry about. It could be losing your spouse, your health, your prestige, or something else that matters to you.

Yikes!

The Law doesn't distinguish between "good" or "bad" experiences. It just responds to the strongest Mental Programs you send.

We talked about entropy and needing to use effort to make changes happen. Paying attention to what you focus on is part of that effort. If you notice yourself focusing on something you fear, then switch your thoughts to something positive as quickly as possible.

We'll get into a little more about how this works in the Absolute Value chapter in the Energy Intensity section.

Getting Clear About Your Desires

The key to experiencing greater success, or having more of the experiences you want in life, is to become more intentional in the Mental Programs you send The Law. Take some time to think about what you authentically want to experience.

What does success mean to you?

What things and experiences would bring you the greatest joy?

What would it take for you to feel more fulfilled or like your life has more meaning?

There is no "right" answer to those questions. That knee-jerk response of wanting $1 million may not be what you truly desire. All of us have a unique definition of what a successful, happy life looks like … *and no two are exactly the same.*

The big house or the fancy car may not be what would make your heart sing. Don't let your desires be influenced by what others think success should look like either. It's important to focus on what you want, not on:

- what you think someone else wants for you
- what someone else thinks success means

- what someone says you "should" be aiming toward in your life or career

We've met far too many people who followed someone else's advice about the career they should pursue. In almost every case, the person is unhappy with the decision and wishes they had taken another path long ago.

Sometimes a person chooses early in life to take the easy option. They choose a career that is something they're good at but have no genuine passion for. The same result happens; they're unhappy and regret the years or decades they feel were wasted.

Deciding what you want can be a daunting task. You might initially think, "I want a house at the beach and a million dollars and a trip to Bora Bora and ..."

But are those really what you want?

When you understand the complete formula, you'll realize that you have to take a fair number of actions to bring in those goals. And, as you've already learned, you must believe that those things and experiences are possible.

The first idea that comes to mind is often not truly what you want. It may be an idea heavily influenced by others through social media, pop-culture, or television. It's important to understand that you can create any experience through The Law as long as you can follow the formula and engage all five components.

Maybe you have a desire for something that you have a tough time believing is feasible right now. Don't let that discourage you from dreaming about a better future. Just because you don't believe something is possible today, doesn't mean it won't ever happen. As you learn and grow, you'll have greater and greater success. Your goals and achievements will continue to become greater over time as well.

Mark:

I didn't stop experimenting after manifesting the luggage cart while on vacation. I intentionally worked with The Law to manifest many additional experiences. A few of those include:

- taking only a few days to find a loving home for my daughter's lame horse
- quickly finding a buyer for the horse trailer we no longer needed
- hitting all green lights when I was running late to a meeting
- finding several new opportunities within the company I worked for

Each positive result solidified my belief even more that The Law was real and helped me stretch what I believed to be possible.

The more success I had, the more I thought about going after bigger dreams. As I thought about various possibilities, I settled on a particular higher-level job within the company I worked for. I set out to become a plant manager.

Soon after making that decision, an assistant plant manager position opened up. I thought it would be a great stepping stone on the way to the position I ultimately wanted.

I applied for the position and set up a time to meet with the current plant manager, someone I'd worked with for many years, to discuss my interest. I felt I'd be a terrific assistant plant manager and anticipated having a great conversation.

It didn't go at all as expected.

When he laughed at my interest in the opportunity, I was shocked. He said I was a strong scientist and technical leader doing a superb job in my current position, but he didn't see me as "plant manager material." He believed my science and process knowledge was why I was so successful. He wasn't confident in my capability to lead the larger organization.

I could have easily felt dejected and given up on my goal. After all, the plant manager, who I knew and respected, had just told me he didn't think I would be good at it. Rather than let his negative opinion destroy my dream, I became even more determined to manifest what I'd set out to achieve.

Over the next few months, I looked at plant manager openings at a few other companies and applied to some of them. But those positions didn't pay what I was already earning, so I didn't pursue them further.

I got super excited when I heard about a plant manager position coming open at the company I worked for. It was close to my house. It would provide an opportunity to learn a whole new technology and manufacturing process.

I applied immediately.

There were some fierce competitors for the position, including the person hired for the assistant plant manager position I didn't get, and several colleagues. There was no way to know if I even stood a chance. I was very excited when they contacted me for an in-person interview.

I went in feeling positive. The interview went well. I developed a good rapport with the interviewers and liked what I saw during the plant tour. I left the interview with a strong sense that I was the one for the job.

The selection process took a while. As days continued to pass hearing no news, I didn't allow myself to get discouraged. I had the opposite happen. I became more and more confident and had a deep inner knowing that the job was mine. Finally, I got the call. My intuitive sense was right. They offered me the position, and I happily accepted.

My happiness was two-fold.

Not only did I get the job I wanted, but I also completed another successful experiment manifesting through The Universal Law of Creation. This time with a much larger goal achieved.

Now I could finally conclude that The Law was indeed real. I had proven to myself that if I just followed the formula, then the goals I set were sure to become reality.

The Law Acts Precisely On What You Focus On

I would soon learn just how precise The Law is. It can get you precisely what you program into it. It doesn't fill in any details that you might assume are obvious. For example, I didn't specifically focus on the type of work environment I preferred, or the attitude of the people I'd be working with, or any of the specifics that I would want in a plant manager position. I just focused on the specific job title.

There was no stipulation in my Mental Program about wanting a supportive manager, a collaborative team, or a workforce that was positive and desired to improve. These were all conditions that existed in the division I had been in. I wrongfully assumed they would automatically be part of any new job I received.

The realization that I wasn't "in Kansas anymore" came all too soon. I had certainly manifested the plant manager position. But all the specific details I had assumed and not specified were completely absent. Yes, I was a plant manager just as I'd wanted. But, I quickly found myself dissatisfied and unhappy.

I asked myself, "Why?"

The reason became obvious ... *deep down, I didn't really want to be a plant manager.*

Being a plant manager appeared to be the very definition of success in the company. It allowed one to lead with some freedom and autonomy to make things happen. Plant managers had performance targets to hit. But they had the authority to lead in their own unique way. Others looked on that position as "the position to shoot for." I realized that I never really stopped to think about whether I agreed with the idea that a plant manager position was the definition of success for me. I realized I had adopted someone else's definition of success.

Even though I was unhappy in the new job, it was amazing and thrilling to prove The Law works even for bigger things. With newfound confidence in The Law, I knew I could manifest a more desirable position. I would now work to manifest a position that would take me out of the experience I'd just created into one more suited to my personal definition of success and where I'd be happier and more fulfilled.

As I pondered what I wanted to experience next, I realized I needed to dig a little deeper to find what I truly wanted. My choice needed to be much more thought out this time.

Exercise:

Jot down in your journal any insights you've gained while reading this chapter.

Write in your journal about some experiences you manifested in the past, either intentionally or unintentionally.

Can you think of times when you got exactly what you asked for and realized it wasn't really what you wanted? Write about it in your journal.

Key Concepts

- You have thousands, possibly tens of thousands of thoughts each day
- Many of your thoughts are focused on what you don't want rather than what you do.
- The Law is very specific and doesn't assume details that you don't provide.

Mirror Mirror On the Wall

We've already mentioned how important it is to focus on exactly what you want. You can't do that unless you are certain about what it is that you desire to have, do, or experience.

How do you go about finding clarity and certainty?

Takara:

I've been "playing with," observing, studying, and experiencing multiple successes with The Law for many years. Along the way, I discovered quite a few techniques that can help manifest your dreams, goals, and aspirations.

A very simple technique that I learned 30 years ago came from Victoria West in her teachings called Prosperity Made Simple. It involves looking at yourself in a mirror and observing how your expression changes as you talk about different dreams and goals.

When you think about specific goals and talk about each one out loud, you will notice yourself smiling more and often talking faster when the dream or goal is something you really want. You'll have more energy, passion, excitement, and joy while thinking and talking about those dreams.

When you talk about goals that aren't truly a heart-felt desire, you are much less likely to be smiling. There will be no excitement or enthusiasm in your voice. You can often see changes in your posture, your attitude, the look in your eyes.

Truth leaves signs … *and you can learn how to read them in yourself and others.* The more genuine excitement you have, the more you can rest assured that the particular dream or goal is one you truly want to experience.

Knowing What You Don't Want

Another brilliant method for figuring out what your true heart-felt desires are is to first get clear about what you don't want.

When Takara teaches her very popular class called Manifesting Your Beloved, she often has students go through the following exercise:

1. Think about every relationship you've had personally as well as relationships you've observed (friend's relationships, your parents, even couples on TV or in movies).

2. Write down everything you've experienced yourself or observed in others that you absolutely know you DO NOT WANT in the new relationship you desire to manifest.

3. Now turn each of those negatives into a positive.

For example, if in a previous relationship you didn't feel that your feelings or opinion mattered to your partner, you might conclude that what you want is: "a relationship in which my partner is a great communicator, really cares about my feelings and opinion, where we are equals, and truly appreciate one another."

Even though Takara created this exercise specifically with relationships in mind, you can adapt it to work for anything you desire to have, do, or experience. Just think about all the things you're sure you don't want relating to the thing you are wishing to manifest. Then turn those negatives into a positive.

Life Assessment

Takara developed a Life Assessment Tool to help you take a snapshot look at the areas of your life that you're satisfied with and those that you'd like to change. It's easy to know the one area that needs the most improvement because we tend to focus a lot of attention there. But we often overlook or fail to notice others that could also use some attention. This tool helps you see your complete life in one diagram. It will help you discover your genuine desires when thinking about things you want to do, have, or experience. Visit this link to get yours: https://www.newscienceofsuccess.com/UYFtools/.

General Specificity

When you program down to the smallest detail, you are usually creating based on previous experience. It's difficult to imagine new things and experiences that you have never had before. While you certainly can be as detailed, descriptive, and specific with The Law as you want, there is also another way to Program that we feel is much more effective. Mark terms it "general specificity" or being "generally specific."

Being generally specific in your Programming may sound contradictory. The core principle behind it is to allow The Law to bring about experiences that you cannot conceive of yet. The Law is unlimited. However, we have limits on what we believe is possible and in our ability to see all the possibilities that The Law could potentially create.

When your Mental Program is very specific, you are telling The Law the one and only way that you want the experience to manifest. There is nothing wrong with specific programs. But the more details you provide, the more constraints you place on what experience The Law delivers to you.

———◆———

Mark:

When I programmed wanting "a plant manager position" I was being specific with The Law. But I wasn't specific enough with the details. While I successfully manifested the position I asked for, the overall experience didn't bring me the happiness I thought it would.

I quickly realized that I didn't think deeply enough about what I wanted to experience and feel before deciding to focus on the plant manager position. Had I looked deeper, I would've discovered that I didn't even want to be a plant manager. I wanted something much more meaningful and fulfilling.

If I'd programmed The Law using general specificity to manifest the new position, I would not have used a specific job title. I would've indicated that I wanted to do work that I enjoy doing with people I enjoy working with in an environment of mutual respect, earning more money than I currently was earning.

How Do You Find the Deeper Why?

In troubleshooting problems in my corporate life, I've often used a problem-solving tool called the five why's. You keep asking why questions until you get to the root of the problem. If you stop before you get to the root, you'll be addressing the symptoms of the problem and not the root cause.

If I'd used the five why's for the plant manager position, it would have looked something like this.

Question (Q): Why do I want to be a plant manager?

Answer (A): Because I want to be in a position of authority so I can make decisions about what to do and how to do it. I want to be in charge.

Q: Why do I want to be in charge?

A: Because I'm tired of being told what to do and how to do it. I'm tired of not having the opportunity to try new things or fresh ways of doing things because they are too different from what the leaders see as the "right" way.

Q: Why am I being tired of being told what to do?

A: Because I want the freedom to explore and experiment with new, seemingly far-out yet potentially great ideas, to uncover and discover new things that provide practical real-world results.

Q: Why don't I leave the corporate world and work for myself?

A: Because I don't believe a scientist with my type of background can start his own business. Scientists like me make their living working in corporate roles just as I have been.

Q: Why don't I believe I could work for myself?

A: Because I don't know anyone like me, a scientist, working on their own in a way that brings them the comfortable salary I make in the corporate world.

The five why's would've told me that what I really wanted was freedom to work on my own. But I didn't think such an experience was personally possible. I didn't yet believe that I could make a living that would pay for my house and college for my children if I worked for myself. I had settled into believing that my only way of being financially secure was to work for a large corporation. But by doing so, it was clear that I would never find the freedom or happiness I truly desired.

It can be difficult to decide what you really want. We live in a world with many distractions and a lot of noise. You'll often hear people talk about how many television stations they have or streaming services, yet there is nothing on that they want to watch.

With all the possibilities and all the surrounding noise, how do you sift through everything to figure out what you truly want?

Meditation is a great way to silence mental chatter. It helps you let go of what you think you know or only what you can see based on past experience and open to greater possibilities.

Exercise:

Jot down in your journal any insights you've gained while reading this chapter.

Make a list of things you do NOT want in your journal.

Download and complete the life assessment.

Did you have any realizations about new things you desire based on what you discovered while doing the assessment? Those usually show up as areas of low satisfaction that you haven't been paying attention to because the thing that needs to shift most gets the brunt of your attention.

Key Concepts

- We often limit our potential because of experiences we've had in the past.
- It's often easier to discover what you truly want by first discovering what you absolutely know you don't want.
- Understanding your deeper "why" can lead to far greater happiness and success.

Silence is Golden

When your mind is as still as a placid lake, you can point your thoughts with laser-like focus any way you want to without a bunch of random thoughts impeding what you want.

It takes both discipline and determination to police your thoughts all the time. We're talking about needing to apply effort to get over Entropy again here.

Certain tools and practices make it far easier to manage. When your mind is quiet and still (vs. a continuous stream of random thoughts), then it is far easier to notice when you are thinking a negative thought, obsessing about a fear, or spending too much time pondering something you don't want.

———◆———

Meditation

Takara:

I've meditated every morning for over 30 years. When I say I have no mind chatter or random thoughts, that's not an exaggeration. I don't know how many days, weeks, or years I'd been meditating when that became a daily truth. What I can say is that I started noticing a difference in my stress level almost immediately upon learning and practicing meditation daily.

There are many ways to meditate and there is no perfect way that works for everyone. Meditation is something I recommend people "sample" ... trying various forms of meditation until they find one that they enjoy. The goal is to help them feel more balanced, centered, at peace, and able to notice and control their thoughts.

The benefits of meditation are many and quite profound. In as little as eight weeks, measurable positive changes occur in the brain.

From Takara's bestselling book, *Peering Through the Veil*, "Research studies at UCLA showed that specific areas of the brain were larger in meditators than in non-meditators. A follow-up study at the UCLA Laboratory of Neuro-Imaging found that meditators have stronger neuronal connections between brain regions and less age-related brain shrinkage overall than non-meditators the same age."[30]

Just as a martial artist trains his body to act as an instrument able to block or deliver a punch with speed and precision, deep theta-level meditation provides the discipline the mind needs to stay focused for extremely long periods and to notice negative thoughts and emotions almost as soon as they begin.

Brainwaves:

To understand how meditation works and why, you first need a working knowledge of brainwave patterns.

We'll be discussing four of the primary ones:

- Beta
- Alpha
- Theta
- Delta

Yes, we realize those don't seem to be in order. It is the order they go in when you go from fully awake to fully asleep. When you are fully awake, having a conversation, feeling stressed or hurried, hyped up on caffeine, experiencing most your day, you are primarily in a beta brainwave state. The brainwaves are oscillating at 12 to 30 cycles per second.

When you calm down, listen to relaxing music, do something creative, have a single glass of wine, feel calm and serene, your brainwaves oscillate at 8 to 12 cycles per second, and are in the alpha brainwave state.

As you lie down to go to sleep, the brain goes from beta to the slower alpha, to theta which is slower still. That is a much deeper state of intense drowsiness. Meditation expert, Stuart Wilde, called this the trance state. The brainwaves oscillate at 4 to 7 Hz when you are in theta.

Finally, when you fall completely asleep, your brainwaves drop into the delta level and only oscillate at 0 to 4 Hz.

While experiencing a deep meditation, the body and mind relax. For the 20 or so minutes a day that the person meditates, the body, mind, and emotions are getting to rest. Depending on the type of meditation, it is equivalent to the rest, repair, and rejuvenation of an additional hour or more of sleep.

At first, the new meditator only feels the level of relaxation and slowed down brainwave activity while in meditation. But after some period (days, weeks, months), that sense of feeling more relaxed, less stressed, and having a slower brainwave happens more and more during the rest of the day, even when the person is not meditating.

The more time you spend in a theta brainwave, the easier it is to notice subtle thoughts, subconscious fears when they arise, synchronicities, and even inspirations from the Universe. Theta helps with creativity, intuition, accessing the subconscious mind, learning, having a greater sense of calmness and wellbeing, improved problem solving, and enhanced concentration. All of those greatly assist in staying focused and using The Law for your benefit. Takara and many other meditation instructors insist that "theta is the place to be." Theta brainwaves create cascades of hormones related to relaxation that assist in physical and emotional wellbeing.

For most people, theta brainwave states are almost impossible to reach without assistance.

Sound is the best way to get the brain into a theta brainwave state for an extended period. Various sound methods (called brainwave entrainment) can help you achieve theta. The three most popular are binaural beats, isochronic tones, or a shamanic rattle/drumbeat. Shamanic practitioners create or listen to a rattle or drum going at 4 to 4 1/2 beats per second. A Stanford University study proved that the drumbeat in that rhythm put listeners into a theta brainwave state.[31]

Takara personally prefers music that has binaural beats embedded below the hearing threshold. Those little beats (sounds) gently guide the brain into a slower theta-level oscillation without you having to listen to a beeping or drumming sound consciously.

Once you have practiced using a tool like a drumbeat or other brainwave entrainment sound over some time (weeks or months), then it is possible to drop your brainwaves into theta on your own occasionally without needing the sound tool.

What used to take years to achieve can happen much more quickly using these tools. They're like shortcuts to a better and more full meditative state.

Mark:

I tried many meditation techniques. I could feel the potential benefits of meditation, but there wasn't one form of meditation that I strongly resonated with. I found that I like guided meditations more than techniques that were more driven by me personally. I found that I became easily distracted by simply focusing on my breath ... *a technique often suggested.*

As I continued to explore various forms of meditation, I discovered that listening to music helped me relax and settle into a calm state of being where the chatter in my mind would quiet down. I found that certain types of music worked better for me than others.

When I listen to high-energy violin music by artists like Lindsey Sterling or Celtic Woman, I can feel the vibrations and energy run through my spine and neck. I feel relaxed and settle into a quieter mental state. In this state of relaxation, I often find that new ideas, inspirations, and profound new thoughts emerge. This leads to potential new target experiences (goals) for the future.

When I focus on a particular experience while in this state of mind, the energizing music that helped me get into that state also serves to help me energize the thought of that experience.

This makes it clear to The Law that it's the experience I wish to have. Energized, focused intent is like sending a full color, high definition broadcast of your desires to The

Law. When you lack focus, it's like sending a fuzzy, easy to misinterpret, black and white program to The Law.

The Water Spring Analogy

When I was young, I used to go with my dad to a freshwater spring near our home. The spring ran strong all year long. It had an unlimited supply available to us. The only limit was the size of the container(s) we took to get water.

If we only took a quart jar, we could only bring home a quart. If we took a gallon jug, we could take home a gallon. If we took a 55-gallon drum, we could take home 55 gallons. Any amount of water was possible to collect, but we could only collect the amount we decided we wanted that day.

The Universal Law of Creation works in the same way as the water spring. The Law can deliver anything you decide you want. It knows nothing of the size or magnitude of the experience you are asking for. Your belief, focus, and energy intensity, or lack thereof, form any limitations that occur as you send out a Mental Program.

As you continue to practice with smaller Programs you believe are possible, you'll become more and more proficient at working with The Law and have more and more success. You'll eventually realize that you can create anything and that The Law is limitless just like the water spring.

Once you decide what you want, believe it's possible, focus on the experience and energize the program. That's the New Science of Success.

Practice

Remember, learning to intentionally create your reality takes practice. No one gets it right every time. So pay attention to your thoughts and when you think about or even obsess about what you don't want, just notice and then stop. No need to get upset with yourself for having negative thoughts … *we all do*. Just let it go. Then, on purpose, think about what you do want instead.

Treat it like a game you're learning to win.

And remember to have fun with it!

Exercise:

Jot down in your journal any insights you've gained while reading this chapter.

Try a couple of different meditation techniques and journal about your experience with each one.

Try listening to several types of music or sounds to see if any help you relax and focus your mind. Mark prefers violin. Takara enjoys the sound of the ocean, water tumbling over rocks in a stream, or other nature sounds.

Key Concepts

- It's easier to focus your thoughts when the mind is quiet.
- Deep meditation helps to slow down brain waves and quiet mental chatter.
- Several sound methods can also be used to slow down your brain waves including music, drum beats, etc.

Energy is Everything

The emotions and feelings you hold are the oomph needed to signal to The Universal Law of Creation that a particular Mental Program is what you want to manifest. Emotions can range from the tiniest hint of fear to jumping up and down with excitement.

Energy Intensity

Figure 9. Energy Intensity

A fire can never happen without a spark.

The same is true of creating without having some emotion or feeling behind it.

The amount of energy (feelings/emotions) behind your thoughts directly impacts how well and how soon the things you focus on become part of your life.

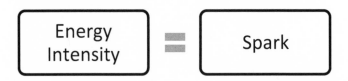

You can have a clear picture of what you want and even believe you can experience it, but if there is no passion or spark behind it, the idea is pretty much dead in the water. It will either never come to pass or it will happen at an excruciatingly slow pace.

Passion, excitement, and other powerful emotions can speed up the manifesting process. The stronger the emotion or feeling, the more intensity it has. As long as all the other components are in place, the more intensity behind it, the faster the mental picture tends to become part of your reality.

Vision Boards

A great way to engage both focus and energy intensity is to create a vision board. As Takara mentioned, she's been using them successfully for 40 years. Many people create a new one in late December or early January ... to focus on the life and experiences they want to have in the new year. They include building a new board with their yearly planning activities.

The basic idea is very simple:

- Decide what you want to have, do, and experience.
- Cut out or print images that represent those things. You can also cut out meaningful words or phrases.
- Put them on a poster board with a glue stick or clear tape.
- Hang your new poster somewhere you will see it often.

Some people hang them in their home office. Others make a small one and hang it on the refrigerator. It just needs to be a place you will see sometimes.

The real power in the vision board is in knowing exactly what you want. You want to take the time to find images that evoke a powerful feeling within you whenever you see them. You need to say an enthusiastic "yes" within when thinking about having whatever the image is about. It is that passion and strong feeling the image evokes that causes vision boards to work so well.

The time you take to find, cut out, and paste the images is time 100% focused on the things you desire. It sends a powerful message to the Universe about what you want.

As with all intentional creation empowerment techniques, your belief in the goal being possible for you matters. If it is a photo of something you don't believe you could ever have, it's best to leave it off the board.

———◆———

Takara:

There are many ways to work with and enhance your vision board for maximum effectiveness.

One way I suggest is to get a metal write on wipe off board and position the pictures on it with magnets rather than glue or tape. Whenever you attain something on the board, replace it with an image of a new goal or desire. A cork board could also work in this case where tacks are used to hold the images in place.

Another idea is what I call "putting yourself in the picture." When I wanted to be a bestselling author, I found a bestseller list online, carefully cut out one of the author's names along with the name of their book, and replaced it with my own. I made sure the font and size-matched … *so it looked like my book and name belonged on that list.* I put the newly "enhanced" list on my vision board. I share the results of this vision board enhancement in a later chapter.

A different way of utilizing the "putting yourself in the picture" idea was when I wanted to speak as an expert on online summits. I found an ad in a magazine for a day-long event with several well-known speakers. I cut out one of the pictures and names and replaced it with my photo (adjusted to the correct size) and put my name underneath. Again I matched the font and size for the name. I stuck it on the wall in my second office. I saw it whenever I walked into the room.

Fast forward a few months. I was staring at an ad for one of the online summits I was speaking at. I realized I was the first speaker in the lineup of presenters ... *the headliner.* I also realized the photos of speakers with their names underneath in the ad looked almost identical to the one I'd put on my wall mentioned above.

This "putting yourself in the picture" technique is powerful. If you want a new home, get a photo of your ideal home and then Photoshop in a photo of you ... as if you are standing in front of your new home or standing by the front door about to walk inside. Photoshop skills are a definite plus. There are free places online you can get the background taken out of a photo so you can then add yourself to another image.

You can do the same thing for a new vehicle. Get a photo of the new car or truck and Photoshop yourself sitting in the driver's seat. Put it on your vision board.

In a previous chapter, Mark shared his story of manifesting a plant manager's position without stipulating other necessary criteria to ensure it would be something he would enjoy.

I have a similar story related to relationship. I was putting together materials and prepping to teach a class on manifesting with vision boards and decided to create a new vision board for myself to show the class as an example. I'd been on the fence for quite a while about whether I wanted to manifest a romantic relationship.

We've already talked about the importance of being sure you really want something. But I digress.

My marriage had been a very magical manifestation and was truly fabulous for five years and then was terrible for five years. I'd had many previous relationships that left me in emotional pain. The thought of potentially going through more heartache wasn't very appealing.

But, sort of on a whim, and because I needed to fill my new vision board with something, I thought about the kind of relationship I might like. I thought about a movie I'd watched many times. When my former husband and I first separated, I watched August Rush practically every night for several months. There was just something about the movie that touched me on a deep level. And, as an introvert who always turned to movies when I needed to replenish my energy, watching it became a form of therapy while I navigated my new life as a single mom.

There is a particular scene in the movie when the two main characters first meet, both of them musicians living in very different worlds ... *she in the symphony, he in the rock world.* He beckons her to join him on a high roof overlooking Washington Square Park in Manhattan. They listen as a street musician plays Moon Dance on guitar and, just for a moment, Jonathan Rhys Meyers stares at Keri Russell as if he can see to the very depths of her soul with absolute awareness and acceptance. The feeling that it evokes in me is truly profound. So, I decided to find a guy who could do "that."

I found a photo of the two of them sitting on the ledge with him staring at her in that beautiful moment and put it on my board. Then in large letters, I typed the words "A guy who looks at me the way he looks at her," and put that next to it on the board. I then added a few silhouettes of romantic couples to complete the romance section of my board.

What did I get?

You guessed it ...a guy who stared at me with that same type of stare ... *a musician no less*. Every time our paths crossed, we would lock eyes and continue doing that again and again throughout whatever function. If he was performing, he would stare at me in the audience noticeably more than he did at any of the other people present. We went to dinner after one of his performances and he kept holding my hand and staring at me like that, even though we had other friends present at our table.

I was helping a friend at her booth at a summer festival. He was there to perform. I looked up from whatever I was doing and saw him walking toward the booth. As he started to walk by, he met some friends walking in the opposite direction. They stood there talking to one another right in front of the booth. Once he noticed me, he stared throughout the rest of their conversation. Afterward, my friend asked, "Who is that?" She said she could tell we had a deep connection. I laughed and shared that we always did that ... *the deep stare as if we'd known and understood one another for eons.*

Later that evening, we went together to listen and dance to the live music being performed on the main stage. We kissed a few times and stood with our arms around one another most of the time. The chemistry was fabulous. We could have easily looked like one of the silhouettes I had on my vision board back home. It was during that evening together that I discovered he had quite a lot going on and wasn't looking for a relationship. He's a great guy, just not dating material for me at the moment.

I got exactly what I asked for.

I had stipulated nothing about the person or the relationship when I put the images on the board, just a guy who would look at me like Jonathan Rhys Meyers looks at Keri Russell in a movie. How silly is that? I was howling laughing when I realized what I'd done.

Yes, The Law absolutely works. And, you really need to pay attention to what you ask for.

---◆---

Ultimately it's about how you want to feel. Every choice you make around what you want to manifest needs to be something you believe will help you feel the way you are aiming to feel:

- happier
- more fulfilled

- safer (often with money desires or wanting to live in a safer neighborhood)
- freer …
- you get the idea

Exercise:

Jot down in your journal any insights you've gained while reading this chapter.

Make a new page in your journal about the things you want to have, do, and experience.

Create a vision board based on those desires. Be sure to choose pictures and words that evoke a deep feeling within of "yes, I really want this." Make sure the things you choose are not too far outside your belief in what is possible for you.

Put your vision board somewhere you will see it every day. You don't have to stare at it daily. Your subconscious will pay attention even if you don't make a point to stare. You just need to give your subconscious mind the opportunity to notice it repeatedly.

You can even take a photo of your board and put it in your journal.

Then make notes about what's on the board. Note when they manifest.

As you learn more about manifesting by reading the remainder of the book, apply what you learn toward the things on your board. Only focus on one thing at a time until it manifests.

Key Concepts

- The energy (feeling / emotion) behind your thoughts greatly impacts what you manifest as well as how quickly it shows up in your life.
- Vision boards are a powerful tool for increasing focus and energy intensity.
- The Law delivers exactly what you ask for.

What's Math Got to Do With It?

Mark:

When first learning about intentional (or deliberate) creation, one concept I had trouble grasping was getting what I want vs. what I don't want. I found it puzzling. If I think of not wanting something, why did the universe respond by manifesting the exact experience that I knew I didn't want?

All the explanations I found seemed to be missing something.

Then, suddenly, the full understanding hit me.

In mathematics, there is a concept known as absolute value. It is the magnitude or distance away from zero of the number regardless of its sign. In an equation, this symbol, $|\ |$, indicates absolute value.

Number Line

-10 -9 -8 -7 -6 -5 -4 -3 -2 -1 0 1 2 3 4 5 6 7 8 9 10

The absolute value of -10 is 10 (10 away from zero).
$|-10| = 10$

And the absolute value of +10 is also 10 (10 away from zero).

| 10 | = 10

Relating this to The Law ... think about the magnitude (how big the number is away from zero) of how passionate you are about whatever you are thinking about most of the time. How much do you hate the thing you don't want? Or, how much do you want the thing or experience you desire? The level of passion or energy behind your thoughts and desires has a tremendous impact on how quickly those things show up.

It was a eureka moment when I discovered that The Law works in absolute values.

If I was thinking about how much I didn't want to work in the job I hated, the absolute value of that thought was translated like this:

| I do not want to work at this job I hate | = I work at this job I hate

When you think about things you don't want, the image in your mind and the passionate energy you feel for or against it is of that experience. When I thought about the job I hated (which I definitely didn't want), the image in my mind was of me working at the job I hate accompanied by the passionate dislike of going to the job every day. Not wanting the experience doesn't exist in my vision.

"I do not want" is merely an add-on unrecognized by the Universe ... *much like the minus sign in an absolute value equation.*

The universe only recognizes the thought you're focused on and the amount of passion you have towards it. So I was shouting to the universe to create the vivid image filled with passion that I was focusing on ... *even though it was something I desperately didn't want.*

The new plant manager's job was not going well. I knew my boss wasn't happy with my performance. The usual outcome for someone in my position in that division was getting fired. I began to worry about that possibility.

I quickly stopped that negative train of thought because I knew The Law would manifest whatever I focused on, believed was possible, and energized even if it was something I didn't want. If I worried about being fired or tried to create "not being fired," it would make no difference.

I found myself working in a place that didn't understand my vision of winning through teamwork. It was frustrating, and I was becoming more and more disheartened with each passing day.

It would've been easy to dwell on how bad my work situation was and how much I hated the new role I'd intentionally manifested. And to be honest, that is where I started. I was in a horrible situation and that was where my thoughts were initially focused. I had clear thoughts of hating my job combined with an intense:

- fear of being fired
- dislike for the job that I had focused on and manifested
- regret for having accepted the position

Thankfully, I realized that dwelling on the things I disliked was not helpful. I needed to turn my thoughts in a completely different direction. I made the conscious decision to apply everything I'd learned through my study and experimentation with The Law. Continuing to focus on what I didn't want would only bring me more of the same.

What was it I really wanted?

I began to think about working in an environment with people I liked and respected and who felt the same toward me. What I wanted was a job that I liked doing. I envisioned being offered a new job that I could easily say yes to.

With these new thoughts came a new passion. I felt uplifted and more positive each day I went to work. The current plant manager experience improved.

I focused on the good rather than the bad.

This helped me peacefully exist in the current role while I focused on intentionally programming The Law with a new work experience.

Again, I began seeking jobs outside the company that appeared to align with the positive work experience I wanted. Invitations showed up inviting me for interviews. I could feel a new position coming. But then I stopped to focus on what I really, really wanted.

Leaving the company I'd worked at for decades wasn't really what I wanted to do. "Why should I have to leave to be happy?"

Quickly I realized, I needed a new intention, one that could bring me happiness and fulfillment within the company I had devoted over 20 years of my life to. I focused my thoughts on a new role within the company that included the details of the type of people I wanted to work with and the type of work I wanted to do each day. I fueled this thought with an intense passion, imagining the joy I would feel when I finally was in a new position.

I deserved this new role. I expected this new role. I believed this new role was possible even though almost every other plant manager who found himself in the position I was in, was fired by this division of the company. I gave no attention to what had happened to others and kept a clear focus on the experience I wanted to create.

Within a couple of weeks of creating this new focused intention, my boss asked me to meet with him in his office across town. When I arrived, the HR manager was there as well. My first reaction was, "this can't be good." I calmly walked into the office and closed the door.

To my amazement, they informed me that I was being re-assigned to a newly created position in the Research & Development group called the Open Innovation Manager.

I would work with people I knew and liked, including an old friend.

It amazed me. This unexpected turn of events was not at all normal for this division. This was usually the moment when the plant manager got fired. The creative power of my thought of a new position had manifested a new position perfect for me just as I had imagined. I was watching my Mental Program unfold before my very eyes.

It felt awesome.

That day I realized in a very personal and profound way how real The Law is and how it can be intentionally Programmed for our benefit. I now had a much deeper understanding of how it works. I realized that if I would've continued to focus on how much I hated my new plant manager job and my fear of being fired, I would've continued to feel miserable and unhappy until I actually did get fired.

I walked away from that office feeling happy. I didn't feel like I had failed at the plant manager position. I knew I'd just demonstrated again that the Universal Law of Creation is real and definitely at work in my reality. I had proven that I could now manifest dreams and goals much larger than a parking space or a luggage bin.

This realization brought me so much joy and hope for the future. I had proven that I could experience anything I chose to focus on, believed was possible, and charged with strong energy intensity. I now fully understood the 3 critical components for consciously Programming The Law and created a triangle to represent it.

———◆———

As we said previously, The Law responds to absolute value. It doesn't distinguish the difference between "I want" and "I do not want." It just recognizes the focus of your thoughts along with the passion (or energy) associated with those thoughts.

| I do not want … | = I want … ."

Be sure that you focus on getting what you want and not on getting what you don't want. When you want to change a situation that you don't like, turn your focus and passion away from what you don't want to continue to experience and focus your thoughts and passions on the new experience you do want to create.

Exercise:

Jot down in your journal any insights you've gained while reading this chapter.

Think back in time and try to find an experience you had that you did not want. Did you unintentionally Program that experience by not understanding the absolute value nature of The Law? Write about it in your journal.

Pay attention to your thoughts. When you notice yourself thinking about, worrying about, or talking about things you don't want, try to stop and refocus your attention on something you do desire instead.

Key Concepts

- The Law doesn't recognize "I do not want" in front of the things you think about.
- Often the things you focus on most clearly and have the greatest level of emotion behind are things you don't wish to have or experience.
- It takes effort to move your thoughts away from what you don't want and toward what you do choose to experience.

Don't Just Stand There, Do Something

Utilizing The Mental Programming Triangle isn't enough to bring a desire into reality. As you've seen in The New Science of Success Formula™ Diagram, there are two additional components needed after you mentally program The Law. The first is taking inspired actions. The other is keeping the faith.

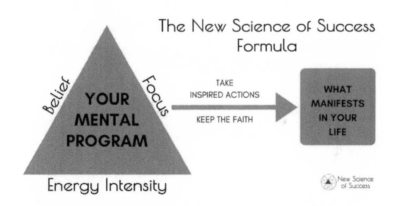

Figure 10. New Science of Success Formula

The bigger the goal, the more actions that are typically required.

You can't decide one day that you want to be a surgeon and expect to begin performing operations the following day. It takes years of dedication, study, achieving good grades, crazy hours as an intern, practice, and mastering precise skills.

If your goal is to start your own business, there are many actions required. You have to decide what type of business you want to have, whether it will be a brick and mortar store or virtual, and so much more. There are nine major areas you need to master to be successful at being an entrepreneur or small business owner. Each of them takes concerted effort to attain and maintain. Takara is working on a book to teach you those.

Mastering a new sport or skill means learning how it works and then practicing. It often involves ongoing work with an instructor or coach. Once you're good enough to play on a team or as a competitor, it will still take years before you're good enough to go pro.

Don't let these things discourage you. It's just how the world works. Few things worth having are easy. The bigger the ambition, the more effort and longer it typically takes to achieve.

Inspired Actions

Inspired actions and regular actions are not the same. Regular actions are the ones you think you need to take because you devised some sort of plan of action to go from where you are now to where you want to be. Sometimes someone says, "this is the way to succeed."

Or, "this is the way it's done," and you develop a plan from there. Simply following that type of roadmap can definitely bring success. But the journey that relies solely on logic can sometimes be long and arduous and often includes numerous unnecessary steps.

When you have engaged the Mental Programming Triangle properly, the Universe sends you signals in the form of intuition or "intuitive hits" as we often call them.

If we go back to the fire triangle analogy, the Mental Program consists of oxygen (belief), firewood (focus), and spark (energy intensity). Adding intuitive actions to the mix is like dowsing the fire with an accelerant such as lighter fluid. It creates a much bigger fire immediately. Inspired actions offer an enormous boost to your manifesting ability.

Takara:

Mark and I originally met decades ago while working in the same town for the same company. He and my roommate were on a softball team together. I sometimes went to games and out to eat with the team afterward. It was at those gatherings that we became friends. As mentioned previously, I left corporate life in my mid 30s. Mark and I were no longer in communication after that. However, I was unaware that he'd been getting my email newsletter for years.

As he worked with The Law and the insights around the Mental Programming Triangle became more and more solidified, he felt compelled to share his findings with others. A book seemed the logical avenue to convey the information. He hired an author coach, but what that person had him doing to write his book just didn't resonate. When he decided to find another one, I came to mind.

He contacted me asking if I'd be his author success coach. People tend to do work with me on many more levels that they initially intended. They come seeking help with their business, their book idea, or because they feel stuck in some way. What transpires is typically some form of life transformation. Mark was no exception.

Rather than getting immediately into the details of the book he wanted to write, in one of our first meetings I was intuitively guided to ask him what he really wanted to do in life ... *if there were no obstacles.*

It was the opportunity for an important seed of possibility to take root in his mind about working for himself and doing charity work, helping a specific group of people. He got to envision a very different life than the one he was currently leading. That became very important later on.

Besides assisting him in envisioning a more fulfilling future, I also helped him with the book. In each of our meetings, he shared more and more of the teachings and the various metaphors and analogies he'd developed to explain The Mental Programming Triangle.

I watched in delight as he transformed. With my assistance, he came to the realization that some of his knowledge wasn't from science but from intuition. And I shared several ways he could use and access his intuition even more.

He blossomed, becoming more and more confident about the insights he was receiving about The Triangle and how manifesting works. His entire demeanor became more mellow. He learned to flow more easily with change. He became more peaceful within and happier overall.

And just in time, because several months later, the company he'd worked for all those years had a major restructuring and he and many others lost their jobs. It was a monumental life change that he seemed to breeze through with flying colors. He already knew what he wanted to do ... *and it didn't involve working at a corporation.*

I'm fairly certain that if he hadn't been envisioning a different path for himself already, the sudden job loss would have been devastating. He jumped into consulting and began to thrive at it pretty much immediately.

The more he shared about manifesting in our meetings, the more I did as well. Eventually, he asked if I would join him in bringing this teaching forth. I'm convinced the Universe was conspiring on our behalf (and yours) even decades ago when the two of us first met. He and I now have the skills, knowledge, and experience necessary to put this information together in a way that can benefit many. Our approach to the material is different. Our skill and knowledge sets are also different. Yet both are necessary for the teaching to be whole and complete.

Mark developed The Triangle. I insisted on the inclusion of taking inspired actions and keeping the faith. From personal experience and helping many others successfully manifest their desires, I knew they were incredibly important in the manifestation process. As we put it all together, I realized that for decades I'd been in training learning how to master all five of the components in the formula. I'd been teaching bits and pieces of it for years. But without the formula, a complete understanding is practically impossible.

———◆———

Intuitive promptings sometimes seem to have nothing to do with your current goals or desires. But by following them anyway, truly amazing *(some might even say miraculous)* things can happen.

———◆———

Takara:

I've always loved the ocean. Living inland, I hadn't been to a beach in a while. I longed for the moist tropical breeze, white sand, palm trees, turquoise water, and the occasional glimpse of my friends with fins, the dolphins.

I had several websites and felt it was time for a visual makeover on all of them. My largest website was so old (created in the year 2000) that I hadn't even used a template. Every single page stood on its own. Global changes to its hundreds of pages were made page by page. I found a gorgeous image of white sand, a palm tree leaning at an interesting angle, and beautiful mint green blending into turquoise water. I sliced it "just right" to become the banner image at the top of all of my websites. Then I had to update each page on every website. It took me weeks to accomplish.

As I mentioned when discussing vision boards, the images you choose have to cause a positive emotion within. Having lived at the beach in Southern California and traveling to many islands over the years, I knew exactly how it felt to stand on a beach like the one in the photo. Spending a few weeks focused on the image, having that euphoric feeling of being there whenever I saw it, I was literally "calling in" the experience.

A week or two after the website makeover was complete, I was working at my desk and suddenly thought of a guy I hadn't thought of in years. I learned a long time ago that whenever I have a stray thought, it's important to stop everything and pay attention. The guy's name was Kelly, and he was an incredible orca photographer. I wondered if he had become more famous, possibly known on the mainland rather than just at his local gallery on San Juan Island … *a place I had lived when he and I first met.*

A quick Google search let me know he had a profile on Facebook. I sent him a friend request. Checking out his profile and website, I learned he'd moved away from the San Juans and about the career path he was now taking. Since I'd paid attention and followed the intuitive hunch, I went back to the work at my desk and forgot all about it.

A few days later I suddenly had another intuitive realization. "Kelly had lived on San Juan Island and I had lived on San Juan Island. It's not a very big place. I bet there are people on his friend's list that I know from there." So I hopped on Facebook and went searching for familiar names and faces. When I came across one in particular, I broke out in a huge grin ... *Brian.*

Oh, what fond memories it brought up. When I lived on San Juan Island, I had just quit my job as an engineer and manager in pharmaceuticals manufacturing and moved there to co-found a non-profit for dolphins and whales. Brian was the Port Commissioner and leased yachts for a living. He would call me occasionally and ask if I'd like to go to dinner. I would smile from ear to ear and say, "Why, yes, I would love to go to dinner." Dinner with Brian always involved a gorgeous boat ride, typically to another island on some amazing yacht. To me, it was the epitome of a perfect evening ... *water, stars, fabulous food, and great conversation.* We had so much fun together.

When I saw his name on Kelly's friends' list, all those wonderful evenings came to mind. I quickly asked to be his friend on Facebook. It had been 15 years since we'd seen or talked to one another. What ensued was a barrage of emails sharing what we each had been up to and the previous events in our lives. I'd married, become a parent, and divorced. He had married, divorced, and become extremely successful in the yacht leasing business.

He shared that his lifelong dream had been to own his own yacht and circumnavigate the globe in it. He had just turned 60 and that lifelong dream was finally coming into being. He was currently in Puerto Vallarta for a couple of months prepping the boat for the big *puddle jump*. That's when an entire armada of boats (some motorized like his and some under sail) would head due west together and not hit land for 15 or more days. He started sending me photos of sand and dolphins and invited me to join him there. I laughed and said, "no," and we continued the email conversation.

Once the armada headed out, I didn't hear from him until he reached the first island 17 days later. As soon as he arrived, he sent me more photos of the tropical beaches there and invited me again to join him on the boat. This continued through Bora Bora and Tahiti and many other islands. I always laughed and said no.

Then one day he sent a message saying he really could use my help. The couple he had on board had to fly back to the U.S. for some tax issue, and it was not a boat that could operate with just one person. I would fly into Fiji, stay on board for about a month and fly home from Brisbane, Australia. I literally broke down in tears. Every fiber of my being wanted to be on that boat and in those locations. I sent a message back saying, "I can't be gone for a month, I have a kid." He came back with, "bring the kid."

And that's how I ended up on a million-dollar yacht in Fiji, island-hopping throughout the South Pacific. Rather than a month, we were there for six weeks. It was the most extraordinary adventure of my life.

The moral of this story is this ... if I had not stopped everything and followed that whim of a thought about the guy Kelly I once knew and then followed another fleeting thought to see who was on his friend's list, I probably never would have experienced the greatest trip of my life. Neither action seemed connected to my dream of being on a beach. Yet both were vital to it coming to fruition in as grand a way as it did.

Actions are necessary whether stemming from intuition or logic. Few manifestations occur without you having to take some sort of action. Often, the bigger the dream, the more, and more uncomfortable, the actions needed.

Taking my child on a plane and flying to Fiji to spend a month or more on a yacht with a guy I hadn't seen in 15 years took guts. So did saying, "yes," to the opportunity when it presented itself. Figuring out how to keep my business running without me meant I had to do all sorts of unusual things. Some would find those challenges too hard to overcome. They would say "no" to such an opportunity. I say this often to clients and students ...

"You have to get comfortable being uncomfortable" if you want your life to change.

If your intuition is a little rusty, or perhaps seemingly nonexistent, we've got you covered. We plan to talk about enhancing your intuition in-depth in an upcoming book.

Doing the One Right Thing

As an engineer and process improvement specialist, I was aware of the 80/20 rule. Eighty percent of improvements happen because of only 20 percent of the actions. The same is often true in manifesting. 80 percent of the results are due to 20 percent of the actions you take. The other actions have far less impact.

I developed a similar philosophy I call, *Doing the One Right Thing* after listening to one of my early mentors, Stuart Wilde, share the following story.

He talked about an event he was hosting in Seattle that was to happen in a few days. He called his publicist and asked how many students were attending the course he was teaching. The response was, "none." He then asked about what the publicist had done to advertise the event. They came back with, "nothing really."

Stuart freaked out a bit. He was flying in and there were no students. If he had been doing his own promoting, he would have put up hundreds of flyers, taken out ads in newspapers and magazines, and taken lots of other actions.

Then the publicist said, "Well, I did do this one thing. I booked you on a live daytime talk show." After the show aired, the class filled to capacity. The publicist had done The One Right Thing that made all the difference. Stuart realized some actions cause much greater results than others.

It has been my experience that figuring out what that one right thing is rarely comes from logic and typically comes through intuition.

In this next example, I marry the two things together.

Becoming a Bestselling Author

I'd always wanted to be a writer. Even as a kid in junior high school, I'd sit for hours with an enormous stack of paper next to one of those big clunky upright typewriters and type away with it. I didn't know how to type, so all the letters were just gibberish. I did it because I loved how it felt to create the pages.

Feeling what it would feel like to have the thing you want is a powerful manifestation tool. This was me feeling what it would feel like to be a professional writer.

Fast forward to 1996 when I left the corporate world and set up my first website. It was for a non-profit I co-founded for dolphins and whales. Through blogging and email, I could write to my heart's content. And then I learned you could be a published author online.

I created my first book many years ago. Thanks to my friend, Mark Joyner, a famous internet marketer who came up with the revolutionary idea of the ebook and in giving them away to get people on an email list, I began creating ebooks. One I gave away to build my email list.

The others to sell for $7 on my website. It was so long ago, I didn't even have an online payment processor. People would download and print an actual order form and send me checks in the mail or U.S. Money Orders if they were from outside the United States. Thousands of people downloaded the free one and the $7 ones sold like hotcakes.

They had no fancy covers or professional editing or special formatting. They were just 8 1/2 x 11 sheets of paper with words and chapter headings created in a Microsoft Word document. I converted them to pdf so everyone could read them. But I had to include instructions on how to download a free pdf reader because not everyone knew how. Oh, those were the days.

As we talked about earlier, who you tell your dreams to matters. My then-husband wasn't supportive of my dreams and goals ... *especially the ones that involved me sitting behind a computer screen for hours on end*. There is no way I could be the success I wanted to be as an author with him by my side.

When the marriage finally ended, I began studying book writing, publishing, launching, and promotion with a lot more vigor and enthusiasm and got much more serious about publishing an actual printed book. I was working on several books at the time but hadn't decided which one to bring to the print market first.

It was about this time that I used the intuitively guided enhancement I shared earlier in the vision board section about adding my name to a bestseller list.

Soon after, I got an email from someone I didn't know saying my ebook *Peering Through the Veil* had won an award. I was quite thrilled, of course. I was surprised as well. Information about the ebook existed somewhere on one of my many websites. I rarely promoted it. The only time people heard about it was through my automatic email sequence. I couldn't figure out how the selection committee had even heard about it.

However, I believe in intuitive signs. So I took it as a sign that the Universe wanted me to publish *Peering Through the Veil* as my first book in print. At the time, it was little more than a booklet describing how to do a few different forms of meditation. It would need a lot of work to become an actual book worthy of print.

Putting on my engineering and project management cap, I studied everything I could get my hands on about self-publishing and created a huge spreadsheet of things the experts say are necessary when launching one. In addition to the main spreadsheet with 450+ line items of things to do, there were additional sheets that went into more detail about a few items on the main list.

Looking at the list was overwhelming. If I took the time to do everything, it would take years to get the book out. Obviously, some prioritization was in order. The idea of doing The One Right Thing came to mind.

I went into a deep meditative state and asked what the most important things were that I needed to focus on. I was intuitively guided to pay attention to three specific things. Whew ... *that I can do.*

However, one of them was extremely hard for me.

I have to share another story so you will understand why I found it so hard ...

When I was in high school, I was the best typist in my typing class. I used "imagining it real" to achieve that distinction. I didn't set out to be the best typist. I just liked typing. So I played a little game in my head. Whenever I saw a sign or slogan of any kind, I would type it out in my mind. Sometimes I would put my fingers on a surface and literally move them as if I was typing. Other times, I did the whole thing just in my mind. Either way, I got better and better.

Years later, I won a typing duel. All the managers at a new plant I was helping to start up had a typing contest to see which of us could type the fastest with the most accuracy. It came down to me and the head of accounting. Being a good typist meant a person could type 60 words per minute with up to 2 errors. I won the typing dual doing 120 words per minute with zero errors. That's the power of "imagining it real."

Back to being the best typist in my high school typing class, that got me a job at the local hospital working the 3 to 11 shift in the Admissions office. One day, the Office Manager said she needed me to learn how to run the hospital switchboard to relieve the switchboard operator for her dinner break.

This was back in the day when every call to anyone in a hospital, staff or patient, went through the switchboard. All the doctors and important staff members had pagers. People would call the switchboard, ask to speak to a doctor and the operator would buzz the doctor's pager. The doctor would then call the switchboard operator to get the message. It was an extremely important job and I got very little training.

The very first night while relieving the operator for dinner, I got a call from a doctor saying, "don't page me until 7" and he hung up the phone. It was years before phones had caller ID, he didn't identify himself, and I had absolutely no idea who he was.

I'm sure you can guess the rest. Of course, someone needed him before 7, and not knowing who he was, I made his pager buzz. He was furious. I grew up in a home where no one ever raised their voice. No one ever yelled, called one another derogatory names, or used profanity. This guy was screaming all sorts of profanity at me. I didn't even know what to say. I couldn't even get out the words, "you never identified yourself."

From that moment on, I found it terrifying to call strangers on the phone. Later, that spilled over into emailing strangers. Reaching out to someone I didn't know, especially asking them for something, was almost paralyzing. I could talk to anyone who called me. I just couldn't bring myself to call someone I didn't know already.

One of the three most important things my intuition indicated I needed to do to launch my book successfully was to reach out to some people, including strangers, and ask them to email their list with my book announcement. I had been collecting names and emails of people who might do that for ages. I'd even written the email requesting their support. But I just could not bring myself to hit the send button.

To have a successful book launch, the people emailing for you have to receive notice at least a month in advance, preferably 2 or 3 months in advance. It got right down to the wire. Thirty days until my book was launching and I still hadn't hit send. It was one of those moments where serious decisions and successes or failures are made.

I literally said this to myself out loud: "You have to do this. No one else can do this. No one else is going to do this for you. It is totally up to you. You've put hours and hours and hours into this book and if you don't send this email, no one is going to know about it." I was crying I was so scared. Yet, when push comes to shove, I refused to give up or be a failure. So, I sent the email.

Quite a few positive things happened because I found the courage to go way beyond my comfort zone:

- The book came in #2 in its category on Amazon, right after Eckhart Tolle and followed by Esther Hicks/Abraham and Marianne Williamson.

- If I'd known that achieving a bestseller status was possible with that first printed book, I would have done a little more, sent a few more of those emails to strangers, and likely hit #1. I never thought I'd hit a bestseller list with my first printed book. I was just trying to figure out how self-publishing worked and assumed that achieving bestseller status was something that would happen many printed books later.
- Because I had success myself and developed a system as I created the launch for that first book, I've now helped many other authors hit #1 on Amazon.
- Finding the courage, which was oh so hard to hit that send button allowed me to break free of the fear of reaching out to strangers. Now it's no big deal to email, pick up the phone, or send a private message on social media. It's no longer something that holds me back.

———◆———

It can be monumentally difficult to go outside your comfort zone. That's why we recommend you begin with small goals, things that don't require actions that are too uncomfortable to take.

The more success you have, the more comfortable you will become stretching a little more each time, doing new things, taking new actions, dreaming, and manifesting bigger and bigger goals.

Exercise:

Jot down in your journal any insights you've gained while reading this chapter.

Try to think of times in the past when you followed an intuitive nudge to take an action. Write about it in your journal.

Can you think of a time when you followed logic, even though intuition was trying to point you in a different direction? What would you do differently in that situation now? Write about it in your journal.

Key Concepts

- Thought alone is not enough to manifest the things you desire. Actions are required.
- Intuitive actions are not the same as logical actions. Intuitive actions are far more effective.
- Doing the "one right thing" or a few key things based on intuition is often what makes all the difference in manifesting your greatest aspirations.

Giving Up Is Not An Option

Most people give up on their dreams far too soon. They get excited about some new idea, a new goal they decide they want to achieve. Then day after day, week after week they work toward that goal.

But if things get hard, they have to learn too many new things, they have to take too many uncomfortable actions, or the goal they set doesn't show up within the timeframe they think it should, they throw their hands up in the air stating emphatically, "I give up," "my life will never change," or, "LOA is a lie." Then they go back to the way life was before and give up on that dream. If they do that enough, they begin to believe they can never change their life and eventually give up on even dreaming.

You can't let that be your story. There are many factors involved in manifesting and sometimes goals, dreams, desires don't show up as quickly as you might like.

Sometimes it can take years to achieve a big goal. Takara's dream as a young teen was to be a successful author. She held onto that dream for decades before having a book in print. She never gave up on the dream. She continued to take actions like writing newsletters and blogs that improved her writing ability. She studied famous authors and listened to experts about how to self-publish successfully. And she took actions, including some that were very uncomfortable, to get the goal accomplished. Even when things got hard, she never let the dream die.

When you are clear about your goal, know for certain it's a heartfelt desire, have let the Universe know about it with your Mental Program (belief, focus, energy intensity), and have taken inspired actions, the next step is to trust that one day some day you'll achieve the goal. You can't get caught up in when that will be. And you can't allow yourself to give up hope.

This is where paying close attention to what you are thinking and feeling comes into play. If you allow yourself to go into a negative thinking spin about it not working, then you will begin creating with your negative thoughts and emotions what you don't want ... *never achieving the goal.*

As soon as you notice yourself slipping into negative thinking and feeling, do whatever it takes to get out of it. Find a distraction that puts you in a good mood:

- Listen to an uplifting podcast or interview
- Read an uplifting book
- Listening to music
- Meditate
- Go for a run
- Dance

- Create something with art (paint, color, sculpt, sew, build something, make something, etc.)
- Call a friend that makes you smile

Do something to get your mind off the negative.

When you feel tempted to give up, read the chapter called You Are Not Alone, reminding yourself that many highly successful people also struggled to achieve their dreams.

Stay Positive

It's not easy to stay centered, balanced, at peace, or positive most of the time. But it can make a big difference in your ability to manifest. Meditation greatly helps in feeling serene throughout the day. In that state, you are much less likely to over-react when the unexpected happens.

Avoiding people, information, and situations that are upsetting can also make a monumental difference. Most people don't realize it, but listening to or reading the news can be highly upsetting. News programs often highlight the worst of what is happening in the world. That causes us to feel that the world is not a safe place, that things can go wrong around every corner. It causes us to live in fear. That doesn't mean you should stick your head in the sand, ignoring what's going on. It just means it's best to stay informed, but not to dwell on the negative.

Staying positive also doesn't mean "stuffing" your emotions or ignoring your genuine feelings, pretending they aren't there. If you get upset about something, take a moment to figure out why. We talked about this in a previous chapter.

For people who lean toward the negative, studies show dehydration plays a big factor in depression.[32] We know how important pure water is to physical health. It's vital for mental health as well. For prolonged depression, get professional assistance.

For most goals, you have to keep holding onto the faith (believing) that they will eventually manifest and keep taking actions toward them even when nothing seems to be happening, or no evidence is present showing the goal is getting closer to being achieved.

Giving up too soon is why most people fail. Those who never give up are the ones who win.

Exercise:

Jot down in your journal any insights you've gained while reading this chapter.

Remember a time when you refused to give up until you had achieved your goal. What made you keep going? How can you apply the lessons learned through that experience to what you want to manifest now? Write about it in your journal.

Key Concepts

- Perseverance is a key to achieving success.
- The Law is universal just like gravity. You can have faith that The Law is always at work.
- When negativity and doubt arise, do whatever it takes to lift yourself into a more positive state of mind.

Manifesting On Demand

The Law doesn't randomly select a Mental Signal to manifest. It acts on the ones that you:

- believe are most likely
- often focus on
- have the greatest emotion or feeling about
- continue to take actions toward
- and never give up on (or continue to worry about)

That's true, even if the focus is on something you don't want.

Figure 11. Radio Signal

The Radio Analogy

It works a lot like an FM radio receiver. If you turn on your radio and search the FM stations, you'll only find the ones that broadcast a strong enough signal to your location. If you live in or near Pittsburgh, PA, you can only pick up stations near Pittsburgh. Signals from cities further away, like Chicago, will not be powerful enough for your radio in Pittsburgh to receive.

Your Mental Signals broadcast to The Law at different strengths. The Law will capture and act on the strongest ones. This happens all day every day, whether or not you are consciously sending signals.

Even before you were aware of The Law's existence, you were sending Signals and Programming it. Sometimes those life experiences were wonderful. Sadly, at other times, you sent really powerful signals by worrying about something you didn't want to happen. The Law received those strong signals and gave you precisely what you had been broadcasting through your obsessive worry. You may have felt like you had no control over your life circumstance, but your thoughts actually played an enormous factor. You've always been the writer, director, and star of your life drama. That's why it's so important to pay attention to your thoughts and feelings and change them whenever and however necessary.

Once you're aware of The Law and understand your role in Programming it, you're now ready to move from unconscious Programming to intentional Programming.

That means deliberately choosing the Signals you send and at what strength. You can intensify the strength of the Signals of the things you want and tone down or turn off those you don't want.

Let's go back to the radio analogy. Before satellite radio, you could only find stations on AM or FM. Where you lived dictated the stations and types of programming available. You were not totally in control of what you listened to. With satellite radio, you can listen to almost anything you want, and it doesn't matter where you are in the world. The program or signal about what you want to listen to is always strong and available for your radio to receive. If you intend to listen to rock music, you can listen to rock music. If you change your mind and want to listen to country music, you change the station and listen to country music. You listen to any music you desire at any moment. Your Mental Signals are like that satellite radio ... *they broadcast all the time.* Your job is to control what you are sending.

The key to experiencing more success, more joy, and more happiness is to accept your role as director of your life experience and become more intentional with the Signals you send. The goal is to always strengthen the Mental Signals you desire most and downplay the rest.

The Alchemy of Intentional Programming

The intensity or strength of the three components in the Mental Programming Triangle determine the power or strength of your Mental Signal. The strength of your belief, the magnitude of your focus, and the level of intensity of your energy and passion for the goal are the levers or dials you can intentionally adjust.

You can look at the strength of your Mental Program using this simple *Signal Strength Formula*:

Signal Strength = Belief Strength x Focus Strength
x Energy Intensity Strength

$$S = B \times F \times E$$

S = Signal Strength
B = Belief Strength
F = Focus Strength
E = Energy Intensity Strength

Strength for each component is rated on a scale of 0 to 10, with low numbers being weak and high numbers being very strong.

Belief Strength is how much you believe the goal, dream, or thing you are worried about is possible for you to have. If you think there is no way possible for you to have, do, or experience a particular goal, your belief strength would be 0. If you absolutely believe the goal is possible for you, your belief strength would be 10. If you are on the fence about whether something is possible, your belief strength would be about 5.

Focus Strength is the amount of time you think about the particular experience or take actions toward its achievement. Your thought strength will most likely never be a 10 as you can't focus on only one thought 24 hours a day. Various techniques help you amplify the strength of your focus:

- meditation (helps you stay focused longer)
- vision boards (help you focus subconsciously in an ongoing way)
- imagining it as if real (amplifies your Mental Signal immensely)

You don't have to be exact with your ratings. If you focus little on a thought, you can rate the strength as 1 or 2. If you are actively focusing on a particular thought, have a vision board or taken the time to imagine it real, you could rate it between 6 and 8. Give a lower number to things you aren't really focused on and a higher number to the dreams and goals you are actively working to focus on.

Energy Intensity Strength is the level of energy, passion, or emotion around a thought or desire. If you obsessively worry about a potential experience you'd rather not manifest, the strength of your energy intensity for that thought would be very high. You would rate its strength somewhere between 7 and 9. If you have very little passion or energy toward a particular thought, that thought would have a lower strength. You would rate it something like a 1 or 2. If you are extremely excited about the idea of having a particular goal or dream, the strength of your thoughts toward it would be somewhere between 7 and 9.

Don't get caught up in over-analyzing the strength of your belief, focus, and energy. The overall strength of each Mental Signal is an indicator of the probability that it will manifest. The stronger ones are much more likely to show up in your life. While the weak ones will most likely not become part of your reality.

When you use similar strength rating criteria for each Mental Signal you pay attention to, you can compare them to determine which ones are more likely to manifest. If you notice that something you want to experience is not being Signaled as strongly as you'd like, you can work on strengthening it and weakening the others (turning your focus away from them) to increase the likelihood of achieving the one you most desire.

To calculate the strength of one of your Mental Signals, you first need to assign a level of intensity number to each of the sides of the triangle: belief, focus, and energy intensity.

Let's consider an example to show how the equation and calculation works.

———◆———

Mark:

I've often thought about working for myself at various times throughout my career. Here's what the strength of that signal looked like 5 to 10 years ago.

Belief = 1 (didn't believe it was possible)
Focus = 1 (gave it little thought or attention)
Energy Intensity = 1 (had no energy behind it)

$$S = B(1) \times F(1) \times E(1)$$
$$= 1$$

The strength of my Mental Signal for working for myself was a one … *it was simply never going to happen at that strength.* The highest strength possible for any mental signal is 1000. But you would need to have a strength of 10 on each of the sides of the triangle to achieve that. While achieving a signal strength of 1000 is unlikely to even be possible, a strength value of 1 is extremely low and highly unlikely to manifest.

If I truly wanted the experience of working for myself, I needed to increase the strength of the Signal I was sending to the Universe about that.

In the world of science, measurement and data are very important. In the world of manufacturing and business process improvement, it's often stated that you can't improve what you don't measure.

Without measurement and analysis to help you understand why you are or are not getting what you want, you're in the dark. Putting numbers into the equation and evaluating the result lets you know what you need to adjust to achieve greater success working with The Law.

To own my own business and work for myself, the equation made it blatantly obvious that I needed to work on increasing my belief, focus, and energy intensity around that goal.

———◆———

As we've said, to experience what you truly desire, you need to become more intentional in your Mental Programming of The Law. You need to increase the strength of the Mental Programs you want to manifest and decrease or eliminate the strength of the Mental Programs that are showing up as experiences you don't want.

By measuring and comparing the strength of your Mental Programs, you'll be able to understand why you have been experiencing the things you've been experiencing. By making your unconscious Mental Programs visible, you'll discover what you need to do to eliminate the ones causing undesirable results. And you can figure out what you need to do to strengthen the Mental Signals of the things you really do want to experience.

Mark:

As I mentioned earlier, about 5-10 years ago I thought about manifesting the experience of working for myself. The strength of my Mental Program (S = B x F x E) was 1. It was too weak to ever have a chance of becoming real.

At that same time, I was sending Signals for other potential experiences. The other Mental Signal I was unconsciously broadcasting was about continuing to work for a large corporation like I'd been doing for decades. This Mental Program looked like this:

$$S = B \times F \times E$$

S = Signal Strength
B = Belief
F = Focus
E = Energy Intensity

$$S = B(10) \times F(7) \times E(7)$$
$$= 490$$

The signal strength of my Mental Program for continuing to work at a large corporation was almost 500 times greater than the one for working for myself. It's not surprising that I continued the experience of working for a large corporation. If I really wanted to work for myself, then I needed to significantly strengthen that Mental Program and weaken the other one.

The Mental Program I had running about working for a large company looked like this:

- Belief: I believed 100% that the only way I could find success and make a living was by working for someone else in a big company. I didn't believe that scientists could be successful or make it on their own.

- Focus: I had a strong focus of not wanting to work for a large corporation. Sometimes I thought about how much I disliked working for the corporation that employed me. The only alternative thought I had was about working for a different large company. Deep down I knew that experience would be just the same as where I was.

- Energy Intensity: I had so many feelings of anger and frustration that I was 'trapped' working where I was. I resented needing to stay there to continue to receive the salary and healthcare coverage it provided for my family. I often felt frustrated by even the smallest experiences of what I felt were blocks to my freedom and creativity as a scientist. Overall, I felt strong negative feelings about most aspects of my job. My energy intensity was high, but aimed in the wrong direction.

I realized I would never experience new levels of success and happiness until I could weaken or eliminate the Mental Program to remain in the corporate world. I also knew that I needed to strengthen the Mental Program for the experience I most desired ... *to have the freedom of working for myself.*

Before developing a true understanding of how The Law worked and how to send Mental Programs intentionally, I felt lost.

I felt more and more stuck in my disappointing corporate experience. Excitement was stirring about what The Universal Law of Creation promised, but I didn't know how to get from where I was to the new place I wished to be.

The experimentation that led to the discovery of the three critical factors of the Mental Programming Triangle not only set me free from the limitations I was placing on myself, it also created a systematic approach and measurable roadmap that will help you get from where you are now to where you want to be.

Today I'm an independent consultant doing the work I enjoy most, working with people I like on a schedule I choose. By intentionally Programming The Law, I was able to strengthen the Signal for working for myself while weakening the competing Signal that kept me in the experience of working as a corporate scientist and leader.

I finally achieved the success and freedom I desired for so long.

———◆———

Exercise:

Jot down in your journal any insights you've gained while reading this chapter.

Choose a current experience you are having (either positive or negative) and trace it back to the Mental Program that created it. Write about it in your journal. Calculate the Signal Strength for that Mental Program.

Analyze your current Mental Programs for things you want. Use the Signal Strength Formula to calculate the strength of a few of them and write about it in your journal.

Key Concepts

- Your Mental Programs are like satellite radio signals. You are always broadcasting something to the Universe.
- There is a formula that can be used to calculate the strength of each of your Mental Programs/Signals.
- Your strongest Mental Signals are the ones most likely to manifest.

Easier Said Than Done

Change and goal achievement rarely occur when you're happy and content with your:

- health
- relationships
- career
- financial situation
- parenting ability

Under those circumstances, you don't have enough motivation driving you to take the actions necessary and do whatever it takes to create or manifest something better.

Few people are happy and content in every single area of life and that's when The Formula and knowing how to work with The Law can be so useful.

Dissatisfaction is a Mighty Motivator

Your current level of satisfaction or dissatisfaction plays an important role in how successful you'll be in making lasting life changes like becoming healthier, losing weight, finding a mate, getting a new job, or achieving some other life goal. The following equation created by David Gleicher and later revised by Kathie Dannemiller shows the importance of your satisfaction level.[33] Gleicher developed this equation to model what it takes for an organization to change.

$$D \times V \times F > R = C$$

D = Dissatisfaction with current experience
V = Vision or focused thought of a new experience
F = First steps of a plan to change
R = Resistance
C = Change to take place

The organization's dissatisfaction with the way things currently are x (times) the vision of how things could be x (times) the first steps being taken toward the new vision has to be > (greater than) the organization's resistance to the change.

The only way that a lasting change happens is if the dissatisfaction is high, the vision strong, and the initial actions effective.

Mark realized the equation can also describe what's necessary for individuals to experience positive change as well. He changed it slightly to this Manifesting Change Equation (MCE):

$$D \times V \times F > R = N$$

D = Dissatisfaction with current experience
V = Vision or focused thought of the new experience
F = First steps of a plan to change
R = Resistance
N = New experience manifests into reality

If you want to change the things you have, do, or experience, it's helpful to understand the various forces involved. Just like the organization, your level of dissatisfaction x (times) your vision for something better x (times) the first steps you take toward that change has to be > (greater than) your resistance to the change.

Resistance can seem insurmountable.

A famous line from Star Trek The Next Generation is, "Resistance is futile." It occurs whenever an alien race called The Borg shows up to take over a ship. They're saying that you might as well give up now because we always win. For many people, it's true. Resistance trips up their manifesting efforts every time.

Resistance is not only a barrier to change, but it can also negatively impact your Programs. It can limit your belief, de-energize your focused thought, and cause you to create Programs that conflict with what you truly want.

You need to recognize, neutralize, and overcome resistance in all its forms whenever it shows up. A few of those include:

- old habits (eating potato chips or cookies every time you watch tv)

- fear of the unknown (those necessary, yet scary, inspired actions you need to take)
- all 9 Veils of Illusion™ (fear, limiting beliefs, judgments, expectations, attachments to outcomes, guilt, shame, blame, victimhood)
- limiting personal beliefs developed earlier in life through experiences and comments by parents, teachers, coaches, friends, spiritual leaders, etc.
- entropy, the universal force keeping you in your status quo
- influence of those close to you who have different definitions of success and opinions about what you are good at and "should" do
- media, social media, and pop culture giving you definitions of success and beauty that are not real and especially not real for you

When resistance to change is high, it's often very difficult to overcome. If you aren't successful at overcoming it, your new goal won't manifest.

As we've mentioned previously, you can create powerful Mental Programs that The Law will manifest as long as you can keep the desired Program stronger than other Programs you also create. Fear and doubt cause you to create Programs that are in opposition to what you really want. The stronger the fear, the stronger the negative Program. Those negative Programs negate the positive ones and make them unlikely to manifest.

Reducing the strength of the resistance you face makes it easier to overcome. Also, lowering your resistance protects your desired Mental Program from self-sabotage.

So, how do you reduce resistance?

One way is to keep your new goal a secret so others don't have the opportunity to tell you it won't work or what a bad idea it is. Or if you share your new goal and someone shoots it down as a bad idea, you can simply ignore what they had to say about it.

Mark:

When I applied for the first plant manager job, the hiring manager laughed at me and told me I wasn't plant manager material. I didn't let someone else's opinion deter my focus or determination. I ultimately applied for and landed a plant manager position. Perseverance and determination are powerful. I understood that the only thing limiting what I could manifest was what I believed was possible. I didn't allow that first rejection to limit my belief that I could be a plant manager.

Some people use the discouraging words of others as powerful motivational fuel for change. If a parent, teacher, or someone else in authority said they would never amount to anything or weren't good at something, they mentally said, "watch me," and become powerfully driven to prove the other person wrong.

You and I are usually our own worst enemies when it comes to change. Not only do we limit what's possible by our limited personal beliefs, but we also hold ourselves back by the status quo. It's easier to keep doing the same things everyday living by repetitive familiar patterns than exerting the effort necessary to stretch beyond the status quo for something new and more exciting.

The Change Equation enables you to see what's needed to realize your dreams and goals. It's also useful in recognizing why change has been so bloody difficult thus far … *or possibly hasn't been happening at all.*

Change of any kind always involves resistance. Even positive changes can be stressful and often involve some type of resistance. Anytime you intentionally create a strong Mental Signal to manifest something new, that represents a life change involving resistance. By understanding the change equation along with how The Formula works, you'll be better prepared to overcome the resistance and successfully manifest what you want.

As we previously mentioned, when considering working with The Law to manifest something new, it's important to be aware of your current level of satisfaction or dissatisfaction as it can affect the result.

It's quite common to hear stories of people making significant changes after experiencing a traumatic event or hitting an extreme low point. Such experiences are an opportunity to inner-reflect and notice just how dissatisfied they are in one or more areas of life. High dissatisfaction is a powerful driver to overcome resistance and make changes happen.

When you consider what you want to intentionally program into The Law, you need to understand how this new potential experience compares to your current one. If you're not significantly dissatisfied, you must have intense belief, focus, and energy intensity plus take the first few actions toward the new goal so you can overcome resistance and increase the probability of your goal manifesting.

Mark:

When I first thought about working for myself, my dissatisfaction with my current career was fairly low. I was comfortable with my job and salary. Therefore, I had little motivation to put in the effort needed to overcome my resistance to change.

Five to ten years ago I felt satisfied with my career and my mental signal of working for myself had a very low intensity. It should come as no surprise that I didn't manifest a new career working for myself.

There is nothing wrong with being satisfied and having your life remain the same. It's simply a choice. If you're happy, that's great. Live your own personal definition of success. Don't chase someone else's dream if that's not what will truly bring you happiness.

The second factor in the Mental Change Equation is a vision or focused thought of a novel experience you want to have. As we've discussed, you must get crystal clear about what you want before you can ever manifest it on purpose. Focused thought aimed at a new goal is also one of the three critical components of the Mental Programming Triangle.

When you expand your vision into a full Mental Program by adding belief and energy intensity, it becomes much more clear to The Law the change, the new experience, you want to manifest.

That leads us to the third factor in the Manifesting Change Equation. You have to take the first few steps toward achieving the goal. You can't just sit back and expect that goal to manifest all on its own. You have to be an active participant in the process.

As we mentioned previously, inspired actions are more effective than regular actions. They're the first steps in your plan to manifest the new dream or goal. They help to catalyze and accelerate your Program.

It's important to emphasize that we're talking about the first steps of the plan, not the entire plan. If you create an entire plan from beginning to end, that plan will develop purely from your collective experiences and knowledge. It will probably only include limited ways your new goal could manifest. You are more likely to fall short of experiencing your vision with such a plan.

Starting with inspired or intuitive actions will lead you to possibilities you would never have thought about on your own. Intuitive actions are rooted in a deeper vision and wisdom that the Universe has, which is not readily available to you through your five senses and conscious mind.

By allowing intuition to guide your first action steps, you're allowing for infinite possibilities. One inspired action opens the door to a new set of potential additional actions that would not have been visible to you without you taking that first inspired step. Takara's story of living on a million-dollar yacht exemplifies that idea.

Sometimes, as you head toward one goal, after a few steps, particularly intuitive ones, a new opportunity or possibility presents itself. Then you begin to head in that new direction toward the new goal … *one you didn't know was even possible*. This can happen again and again as you work toward a large goal. If you stick with a strictly logical step-by-step plan from beginning to end, you might achieve the original goal, but completely miss the extraordinary opportunity of achieving something so much better.

Mark:

The plant manager position that turned out so badly is one I had felt intuitively guided to take. Others strongly encouraged me not to apply for or accept it. But intuition disagreed. Years later, I could see how taking that first intuitively guided action was absolutely necessary for the later opportunities to unfold the way they did. That first step, however unpleasant, started an avalanche of magnificent possibility. None of which I could have imagined or experienced had that first step not occurred.

After the tumultuous plant manager position, I was given the newly created Open Innovation Manager position. Serving in that position for three years, I learned new skills and developed expertise in new emerging technologies in the industry. When I first left the corporate world and began working for myself, that newly acquired expertise became a prime focus of my consulting business.

The more success I had with The Law, the more I allowed myself to want, and eventually believe, I could work for myself. My current success as a consultant and entrepreneur was not something I could imagine as a possibility before I walked through that first door opened by taking an inspired action to be a plant manager.

———◆———

Takara:

As Mark and I were developing the concepts for this book, an opportunity showed up for a 3-day virtual event with Susie Carder. I consider her the power behind the throne of Lisa Nichols. She's the reason Lisa's name became so big and her business so successful. I've loved her work for several years and was excited to go. I also got a strong intuitive "hit" that both my son, Jess, and Mark should attend as well.

My son trusts my judgment and decided to attend ... *mostly because mom thought it was a good idea.* He's an aspiring fiction author working on several story ideas.

Mark is a person who makes his own decisions. I wasn't sure if Susie's style would resonate with his logical scientific approach to most things. Working with me over the years, he's learned to follow intuition more and more. When he "tuned in," he got that he should attend.

The things that came out of that 3-day event were phenomenal for both of them. Because it was virtual, there were opportunities to speak to the entire group with questions or comments. After Jess commented about something during one session, someone wrote in the chatbox that he had an incredible voice and should do audiobooks.

I've been making that same suggestion for a few years. But when it's mom saying something about your talents or skills, it's not always believed. Because someone else said it, he heeded the advice. One of my dear friends does book narration professionally. She offered to be his coach and teach him how that business works. They've met several times and he's now pursuing the opportunity. It may never have happened had he not attended the event.

Mark not only attended, but got involved further with Susie's work, and is now facilitating one of her groups. He's also collaborating with someone he met there, working on a project he's wanted to do for years.

I followed my intuition to invite them. My son trusted me. Mark took part because he followed his intuition. And magic happened.

You have to keep the faith that your dreams and goals will manifest while taking inspired actions and acting on the new possibilities that reveal themselves because you took those inspired actions. These activities are necessary to allow the universe to build your life experience in the image of your Mental Program.

The Garden Analogy

Think of it like planting a garden. You have total faith in the laws nature uses to make your plants grow. You know your role is to plant the seed (your Mental Program) and provide sunlight, water, and fertilizer (your inspired actions) to enable and allow the laws of plant growth to transform your seeds into beautiful flowers or delicious vegetables.

You decide what you want, you plant the specific seeds for what you want by creating a strong Mental Signal, and you take the actions of watering and feeding your seeds as they germinate and grow. You hold on to the belief that the seeds will grow even though it takes a while before you see any proof in the form of a baby plant. You know without a doubt that if you do everything following the laws of plant growth, the planted seeds will grow and develop. The Universal Law of Creation works with your Mental Programs with the same precision and reliability as the laws of plant growth work on your planted seeds.

Exercise:

Jot down in your journal any insights you've gained while reading this chapter.

Think of a significant change you made in your past. In your journal, list the forms of resistance you faced and how you overcame them.

Reflect on a time when you took an action based on a gut feel or intuitive hunch. Looking back on it, where did that action ultimately lead you to? Write about it in your journal.

Key Concepts

- Change can be hard. It takes focus and effort to overcome resistance to change.
- Change requires that you take new and different actions.
- Programming The Law is like planting a garden. Even though you can't see anything happening above ground, you have to trust that as you water and care for the seed you've planted, it will grow.

Now It's Your Turn

By teaching you the New Science of Success Formula™ and how to master each of its components, we've handed you the keys to your own manifesting kingdom. It's now time to go out and achieve your dreams.

Clearly Indicate Your Desire

Once you have a specific goal, you must be crystal clear about which Mental Signals you want the universe to pay attention to vs. the thousands of others you broadcast each day.

Here are a few ways to bring more attention to a specific goal you want to manifest:

1. Write it down.
2. Say it out loud.
3. Close your eyes and imagine it in your mind's eye (creating a picture).
4. Feel how it would feel to have the item or experience.
5. Put it on a vision board that you will see often.

Certain ways of writing or stating your goals are far more effective than others.

Visit this link and download our Goal Writing Blueprint:
https://www.NewScienceOfSuccess.com/UYFtools.

As mentioned earlier, it's unrealistic to expect that you will have and hold only the one thought of the goal you want to manifest. It's both realistic and necessary to continue to bring your focus back to what you desire and away from what you don't.

It is also important to learn to recognize when you are focusing on negative, undesirable, thoughts. As one of Takara's mentors, Stuart Wilde, used to say: "You have to constantly skim the lake." That means paying attention to your thoughts and feelings and getting rid of those that are not in alignment with your desires.

When you notice negative feelings and emotions, follow those feelings back to the thought that is generating them. Shift your focus away from that thought and replace it with the thought of your desired experience or with a positive affirmation.

It can also be helpful to combine this shift in thought focus with something that evokes a positive feeling within. For Mark, that something is listening to music.

Focusing your thoughts on what you want while holding a strong positive feeling toward your goal or desire takes practice and will develop over time. Don't be hard on yourself or set unrealistic expectations as you develop those skills. Keep practicing and be persistent. Before you know it, you'll be an exceptional intentional creator.

Living the life of your dreams doesn't happen by accident. Success isn't something reserved exclusively for others. You can be, do, or experience anything you desire. The only thing standing between you and that life is you. The Universal Law of Creation is real. But it requires that you clearly broadcast what you want, take the necessary actions to make it happen, and keep believing until it manifests.

Unleash Your Future has given you a better understanding of how The Law works, along with a formula to intentionally work with it to create the life of your dreams. You are now ready to dream bigger, Program more intentionally, and take the necessary inspired actions toward whatever you choose.

———◆———

Mark:

Once I had expanded my belief in what's possible and solidified my understanding of how The Law works, I was ready to begin intentionally Programming it as a daily practice. The Law went from being a kind of fantasy to a rock-solid reality.

Having a new understanding of how my reality gets created helped relieve many of the stresses I felt and gave me a deep sense of peace, comfort, and personal empowerment.

My new life as an independent consultant didn't come about by accident. I followed the formula and created my success. What just a few years ago felt downright impossible, is now my daily life experience.

As my confidence in The Law grew over time through a succession of smaller wins, it ultimately felt believable and achievable that I could experience working for myself. My life of freedom and independence was no longer out of reach.

My Vision

I started by creating a clear mental picture of what it would feel like to be living a life where I worked for myself. I focused the image on the first Monday morning of my new career and how it would feel to do whatever I wanted that morning. I didn't need to wake up early to go into an office. I could sleep in, or sit outside and enjoy a cup of coffee without feeling rushed, or I could drive my daughters to school, or I could go for a run. Whatever I felt like doing, I could do. This was the symbolic picture in my mind of the freedom I desired.

My intentional Program was set. I now believed that it was possible to work for myself. I focused my thoughts on being an independent consultant and away from thinking about not wanting to work for a large company. I energized the thought with imagining how I would feel that first Monday morning of my new life.

I began taking new actions. I reached out to a former colleague who'd left corporate life and became a consultant. As I listened to his experiences, I could see even more clearly how I could do that too. He shared a book that outlined the important things to do if you wanted to be a successful consultant. It became a helpful roadmap for the new career I'd chosen. I'm confident the book you're now reading will be the powerful roadmap you need to step into your genuine power as the creator of your life.

I contacted people in my network more proactively to check-in and have a conversation. I learned from the book how important it was to network with others to develop potential client leads. I practiced writing proposals for consulting work agreements even before I had anyone to send them to. I was acting as if I was already an independent consultant.

As I focused on this new life that I wanted to experience, the focus on my current career began to fade. I spent much less time and energy lamenting working in a job I disliked. As I let go of the focus on my current work situation, I felt much more at peace. I could feel my desired consulting career coming ever closer and becoming more real.

The strength of my Program for this experience had drastically increased from what it was a few years earlier. Previously, the Mental Program about working for myself looked like this:

$$S = B(1) \times F(1) \times E(1)$$

$$= 1$$

It was now this:

$$S = B(9) \times F(7) \times E(7)$$
$$= 441$$

The strength of my Program for being a consultant was now over 400 times greater than it was a few years earlier. At the same time, the Program for thinking success was only possible in the corporate world decreased from a score of 490 to only 18.

$$S = B(2) \times F(3) \times E(3)$$
$$= 18$$

It was a reduction in the strength of that counter-program by over 25 times. I was now intentionally making it clear to the universe what I wanted. I had successfully strengthened all three sides of the Program Triangle around being a consultant and working for myself.

It wasn't a surprise when the Program I'd been sending became my new reality. I had the opportunity to leave my corporate career in a way that would not negatively affect my family. I could continue to have affordable healthcare along with receiving some seed money to ease any financial worries during the transition to my new career as a consultant.

That first Monday after I left the corporate world felt just as good or better than I envisioned. I sat outside and had a cup of coffee without feeling rushed. I went for a run at a time when I used to be in the office. I had nothing I needed to do. I was free to work or not work at my discretion. I was finally experiencing the freedom I had wanted for so long. The Monday morning I'd been imagining had become real.

Within the first month, I had my first client. I had a second client by month three. I felt at peace. There was little to no stress any more. I had greater confidence in The Law. My life experience was unfolding just as I had Programmed it. I had finally been able to remove the limits on my belief boundaries and was now living the life of my dreams.

The more experiences I create by intentionally Programming The Law, the more my band of personal belief grows leading to even bigger new experiences of success. Intentionally Programming The Law has become my new way of life. It's less stressful and more successful.

Now let's look to your future. You are no longer unaware of your power to create through your thoughts and actions. You now recognize that your thoughts become your reality through an energy transformation process we call The Law. You also know that the Mental Programs you broadcast are at the heart of that process.

While it's extremely helpful to have this model to describe how it works, knowledge alone changes nothing. Theory without practice (experimentation) is nothing more than a collection of words on a page. No scientific principle becomes real or makes a real-world impact without application.

To change your life and experience more of what you want, you need to accept The Law and begin to consistently, consciously, and intentionally work with it. It takes patience, practice, and perseverance.

Your choice is not whether or not to use The Law, for The Law is a universal principle and always working. Your choice is only whether you will fully embrace it consciously and begin to intentionally Program it to transform your life in ways that are more to your liking.

When you decide to fully accept, embrace, and work with The Law, you'll begin noticing areas that need improvement. You'll realize when you need to put in extra effort to strengthen your Programs. You'll start to recognize when you need to work more on belief, focused thought, energy intensity or some combination of the three.

The Baseball Analogy

The game of baseball offers the perfect analogy to bring it all home. The game itself is essentially the same from t-ball all the way through to the major leagues. There are specific sets of skills and sub-skills that players must develop and master to become more and more proficient. These skills include hitting, throwing, catching, running, etc.

Becoming a better player happens through hard work and practice. Players have ups and downs, but with continued practice and perseverance, they continue to improve. The more dedication, effort, and practice they put in, the better they become. The most dedicated, hard-working players are the ones who make it to the major leagues (the professional level).

The road between t-ball and the majors is littered with players who had the potential but ultimately didn't make it. Some of the reasons include:

- Listening to negative comments of others like, "Hey kid, you're terrible," on a day they had a bad game or were just learning.
- Not putting in enough time and effort practicing the core skills to improve their game.
- Starting with above average natural ability and thinking that their natural ability will always carry them to greater and greater levels of success. They never really develop the understanding of the key

skills and how they can work to develop them to get even better.

- Trying to do it alone without listening to their coach.

If you look at working with The Law like developing into a professional baseball player or developing any skill, then you are initially set-up for success. Too often when people first see or hear about The Law, they think that they can immediately hit a home run so to speak. So they choose to target some enormous experience to manifest (often this is $1 Million).

This approach is like barely learning to play t-ball and the next day expecting that you can go directly to the major leagues, step into the batter's box against a 99 mph fastball, and hit a home run. Similarly, the chances of you manifesting $1 Million immediately after you first learn about The Law are essentially zero percent.

Becoming successful with The Law involves having a thorough understanding of the New Science of Success Formula™. It requires that you understand the three critical factors of the Mental Programming Triangle and how to strengthen them. It also means taking inspired actions and keeping the faith knowing and believing that with perseverance will come success, even if the success isn't apparent at first. It requires that you practice and work with all the components of The Formula to strengthen your skills and get better and better at manifesting.

With this knowledge and understanding, you are ready to develop from the t-ball level of manifesting into a major league manifester.

With knowledge comes responsibility. Since you now know how to work with The Law, there's no turning back to your former unconscious and random way of living. All your dreams and goals are now within your grasp. To make these desired experiences your reality, it is time to move to a more intentional engagement of The Law through the systematic approach you've just discovered here.

The pace at which you decide to move forward with more intentionally engaging The Law is entirely up to you. There is no right or wrong here. It is important to just start moving the ball forward. If right now you can't believe your dreams are possible, then pick an experience that is just outside of your current boundary of personal belief but in the direction of your dream experience. Choose something you believe is personally possible for you.

Once you choose a goal and focus your thoughts toward that goal, it's time to take action. And remember, new actions will lead you to the new experiences you desire to manifest. Tune into your intuition. Actions inspired through your intuition open new doors leading to profound possibilities. It may feel uncomfortable at first. But feeling uncomfortable when you stretch outside your comfort zone is perfectly OK. Don't let this slow you down or stop you. The more you trust your intuition to take inspired action which leads to new, desired experiences, the more comfortable you will feel in continuing to tap into your intuition. Small wins and small successes will help your confidence grow which will lead to you stretching your boundaries even further.

Action by action, experience by experience, you will march forward toward your dream experiences.

———◆———

Mark:

I sometimes feel like pinching myself. A few years ago, I couldn't believe that I could experience the success and the reality that my life is today. But as I look back over the past few years, I can see how I got here. I got here by developing and integrating the intentional and systematic use of The Law as a way of life. I can see how my confidence in practically using The Law has grown with each small win and each new experience I intentionally manifested in my life. You can and will do the same thing, but you must first decide to become more intentional in your approach to life and your use of The Law. You must decide to make the intentional programming of The Law a way of life.

———◆———

So what does an intentional use of The Law look like? It starts with intentional Mental Programs. You decide what you want to experience and then you consciously and intentionally create your Mental Program for that experience. With the clear and focused program in place, it's time for action. And as we continue to emphasize, look to your intuition to gently guide you to inspired actions.

At this point, a scientific approach can be a helpful guide. Scientists use a structured approach known as the scientific method to investigate the world around them to make discoveries and further develop the understanding of how our world works. They do this by designing experiments and analyzing the results to draw conclusions. Based upon those conclusions, they develop new understandings which lead to improvements in our daily lives and serves to spark new ideas and new experiments.

When you think about it, you do this same thing every day whether or not you are consciously aware of it. So, what do we mean when we say this? You are always deciding to take various actions. Often you do it on autopilot. Think of the actions you take as experiments. Each action leads to some result. For example, you have a friend who says or does something and you respond. Your response is an action even if it feels more like a reaction. A reaction is an action taken with little to no thought based on past patterns and experiences. If you do the same thing over and over again, you will get the same or similar results. To think otherwise is Einstein's definition of insanity.

Your reaction will spark a response from your friend. This response is now new information that you've gained as a result of your action (experiment). Being intentional would look like you now stepping back and taking time to analyze the result of your action. You would ask questions like, 'is this what I intended to evoke?' or 'I don't feel good about that response, why?' or 'I think my words were misunderstood.' You would analyze the result and draw a conclusion. From that conclusion, you would think about your next step or action. You would consciously think about and intentionally craft your words before responding. The intent of your response would be to steer the overall experience with your friend in that direction that brings you the peace, happiness, and success you desire which is also in alignment with the best interests of your friend.

When you are not being intentional, you may not even think about your friend's response and just react without thinking. This approach leads to random results and can often create conflict and unnecessary stress. When your emotions go negative, they send your thoughts in that same negative direction. Before you even realize it, you've started sending a negative Mental Signal beckoning the Law to give you something you don't actually wish to experience.

There is an Intentional Cycle you can use to help stay on track and successfully create the life you desire. It works like this:

1. Decide what you want.
2. Set your Mental Program, engaging strong belief, focus, and energy.
3. Take an action toward the dream, goal, or desire (1st box below in the Intentional Cycle Diagram).
4. Notice the result of the action (2nd box below in the Intentional Cycle Diagram).
5. Analyze the result of the action you took (3rd box in the Intentional Cycle Diagram).
6. Integrate what you learned by deciding if the action resulted in a good outcome or one you want to change.
7. Repeat starting with number 3.

The diagrams below show you the difference between being intentional and remaining in the status quo. The Intentional Cycle (top image) helps you continuously develop, grow, and move forward … *climbing your mountain of success*. The autopilot Reaction Loop (bottom image) leads to stagnation and entrapment in a life you don't enjoy and wish you could change.

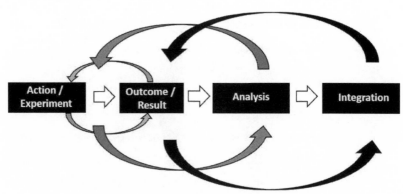

Figure 12 Intentional Cycle

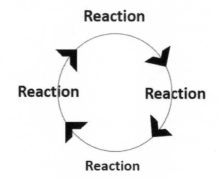

Figure 13. Reaction Loop

The Law is always at work transforming the strongest of your Mental Programs into your daily life experiences. As we've emphasized many times, this is happening even if you aren't consciously aware of it.

When you are not being intentional with your Programming, you get caught up in the Reaction Loop, producing the same type of experiences repeatedly. If you remain in the loop, continuing to do the same things over and over again, then you shouldn't be surprised that you continue to have the same type of experiences again and again.

You can break out of this reactionary, status quo cycle by becoming more intentional with your Mental Programming of The Law. If you want to experience more success and abundance in your life, you need to clearly communicate what you want to the Universe. This focused communication to the Universe makes it clear to The Law those Mental Programs you wish to manifest as your life experience.

The keys to making your desires more visible to the universe are to:

- Reduce the number of Mental Programs you communicate to the universe.
- Significantly increase the strength of the Mental Programs you truly desire by strengthening the intensity of the three critical components of focus, energy intensity, and belief.
- Be mindful of competing and counter Mental Programs and proactively weed these programs out of your mental garden.
- Take inspired actions toward the goals you want to manifest.
- Consciously and continuously analyze the feedback you are receiving through the results/outcomes you observe after taking each action.

- Integrate what you've learn by analyzing the result of previous actions into the planning and execution of future actions.
- Keep the faith that The Law is always at work and that your intentional programming combined with inspired actions will result in your Mental Program being transformed into your life experiences.

The Law works consistently, predictably, and reliably. When you intentionally strengthen the Programs of the things you want and eliminate or significantly reduce the strength of counter Programs (the ones you don't), you should have 100% confidence that the things you want will become part of your life experience.

Exercise:

Jot down in your journal any insights you've gained while reading this chapter.

Download the fill-in-the-blank New Science of Success Formula sheet so you can evaluate the strength of your Programs. You can also simply draw the formula in your journal and fill in the information there Visit this link to get it:

https://www.NewScienceOfSuccess.com/UYFtools.

Key Concepts

- Change can be hard. It takes focus and effort to overcome all the resistance you will face.
- To successfully accomplish change, you have to take new and different actions that are sometimes uncomfortable.
- Learning to manifest successfully is like anything else, the more you practice, the better you get.

Final Thoughts

This is an exciting time in your life. It is a new beginning filled with hope and infinite possibilities. You have everything you need to turn your desired possibilities into the highest probabilities of what you will experience. You're now empowered to live the life of your dreams. You know the rules of the game and how to create success and abundance. It's time to start playing to win big!

Nothing is impossible for you with The Law. Intentionally programming The Law by understanding the New Science of Success Formula, the three critical factors, taking inspired actions, and keeping the faith is your recipe for success. Consistently using this Formula will always lead you to what you desire.

The only limitations on what you can and will experience come from within yourself. It's your time to dream bigger, think more intentionally, believe in yourself, and take inspired action to make the life of your dreams the life you experience day in and day out.

The world is your oyster. May you create the pearls of your dreams through the New Science of Success and the Universal Law of Creation.

Your Game Plan For the Future:

Continue to keep notes in your journal of the goals you set and the successes you have.

Periodically reread the book. The more you experiment, the deeper your understanding will be. As you grow and evolve, you may find insights that you didn't notice the first or even second time you read it.

If your experiments aren't all successes:

1. Ask yourself if the dream or goal is truly a heartfelt desire. Review the Mirror Mirror on the Wall chapter to help you decide.
2. If the answer to (1) is no, drop the goal and choose another.
3. If your answer to (1) is yes, then fill in a blank formula sheet and decide what specific component of the formula needs more attention. Get your blank formula sheet here: https://www.NewScienceOfSuccess.com/UYFtools
4. Do you need to strengthen your belief, take more inspired actions, focus more on the goal rather than something else you fear or are worried about, etc.? There are chapters throughout the book that will help you make those determinations.
5. Visit our website for more tips and tools: https://www.NewScienceOfSuccess.com.

References

1. Hill, Napoleon, and Ross Cornwell. *Think and grow rich!* San Diego, CA: Aventine Press, 2004.
2. "The Secret." IMDb. IMDb.com, September 13, 2007. https://www.imdb.com/title/tt0846789/.
3. Holmes, Ernest. *The Science of Mind: A Philosophy, a Faith, a Way of Life, the Definitive Edition.* New York, NY: TarcherPerigee, 1998.
4. Hill, Napoleon, and Ross Cornwell. *Think and grow rich!* San Diego, CA: Aventine Press, 2004.
5. Gawain, Shakti. *Creative Visualisation.* Whatever Pubs., 1978.
6. Pasha, R. (2016, April 14). The inspiring sylvester stallone success story. Retrieved February 28, 2021, from https://succeedfeed.com/the-inspiring-sylvester-stallone-success-story/
7. Jones, P., Jones, W., & Jones, P. (2016, May 13). How Oprah Winfrey OVERCAME FAILURE. Retrieved February 28, 2021, from https://www.thejobnetwork.com/how-oprah-winfrey-overcame-failure/
8. Gillett, R. (2015, October 07). How Walt Disney, Oprah Winfrey, and 19 other successful People rebounded after getting fired. Retrieved February 28, 2021, from https://www.inc.com/business-insider/21-successful-people-who-rebounded-after-getting-fired.html
9. The Oprah Winfrey Show. (2021, February 17). Retrieved February 28, 2021, from https://en.wikipedia.org/wiki/The_Oprah_Winfrey_Show
10. Oprah Winfrey. (2021, February 28). Retrieved February 28, 2021, from https://en.wikipedia.org/wiki/Oprah_Winfrey
11. Arnett, B., & Watt, J. (n.d.). The unbelievable life of j.j. watt. Retrieved February 28, 2021, from https://www.nfl.com/news/sidelines/the-unbelievable-life-of-j-j-watt

12. Diaz, C., & Cheyenne Diaz Cheyenne Diaz is a Mindvalley Writer. (2020, June 03). Lisa Nichols on why She's helping Millions find their VOICE, speak their truth, and transform their lives. Retrieved February 28, 2021, from https://blog.mindvalley.com/lisa-nichols/

13. Rao, C. (2020, March 14). Was Michael Jordan really cut from his high school basketball team? - Sportscasting: Pure sports. Retrieved February 28, 2021, from https://www.sportscasting.com/was-michael-jordan-really-cut-from-his-high-school-basketball-team/

14. Michael Jordan Quotes. (n.d.). Retrieved March 01, 2021, from https://www.brainyquote.com/quotes/michael_jordan_127660#:~:text=Michael%20Jordan%20Quotes&text=I've%20missed%20more%20than%209000%20shots%20in%20my%20career,over%20again%20in%20my%20life.

15. Howard, J. (2017, December 07). 10 surprising facts About Albert Einstein. Retrieved March 01, 2021, from https://www.huffpost.com/entry/abert-einstein-facts_n_3987801

16. The Nobel Prize in physics 1921. (n.d.). Retrieved March 01, 2021, from https://www.nobelprize.org/prizes/physics/1921/einstein/biographical/

17. Eddie Hall quotes. (n.d.). Retrieved March 02, 2021, from https://www.brainyquote.com/authors/eddie-hall-quotes

18. *Eddie Hall Talks "MENTAL HEALTH"* [Video file]. (2019, March 27). Retrieved March 2, 2021, from https://www.youtube.com/watch?v=k54Mm-z7FrE

19. BREAKING: Eddie hall Makes history, becomes first man to Deadlift 500kg. (2018, October 17). Retrieved March 02, 2021, from https://barbend.com/eddie-hall-makes-history-becomes-first-man-deadlift-500kg/

20. Charles Darwin's school days. (n.d.). Retrieved March 01, 2021, from https://newlearningonline.com/new-learning/chapter-2/supporting-material/charles-darwins-school-days

21. Horbelt, S. (2019, March 01). NYU students had a Facebook group dedicated to bullying an Up-and-Coming Lady Gaga. Retrieved March 01, 2021, from https://hornet.com/stories/lady-gaga-bullying-facebook-group/

22. Aten, J. (2020, December 31). Netflix's most popular show is an overnight success that took 30 years to make. Retrieved March 01, 2021, from https://www.inc.com/jason-aten/netflixs-most-popular-show-is-an-overnight-success-that-took-30-years-to-make.html

23. Abraham Lincoln's "failures" AND "SUCCESSES". (n.d.). Retrieved March 01, 2021, from http://www.abrahamlincolnonline.org/lincoln/education/failures.htm

24. Article by: Gregory Christina Gregory, Christina. "Five Stages Of Grief - Understanding the Kubler-Ross Model." Psycom.net - Mental Health Treatment Resource Since 1996, September 23, 2020. https://www.psycom.net/depression.central.grief.html.

25. Fox, Lisa. "Scarred For Life: The Epigenetics of Fear," October 30, 2018. https://www.whatisepigenetics.com/scarred-for-life-the-epigenetics-of-fear/

26. Orloff, Judith. The Empath's Survival Guide: Life Strategies for Sensitive People. Boulder, CO: Sounds True, Inc., 2018.

27. Becker https://www.success.com/author/jill-becker/, J. (2015, November 30). Shaping Sara Blakely: Meet the billionaire founder of Spanx. Retrieved February 07, 2021, from https://www.success.com/shaping-sara-blakely-meet-the-billionaire-founder-of-spanx/

28. (n.d.). Retrieved February 07, 2021, from https://manifesting.com/ Study conducted by Inspire3, on behalf of Manifesting.com. Yes | No | Unsure question answered by 3129 self-declared Law of Attraction users. Individuals were asked: "Do you get the results you expect when using the Law of Attraction?" 2944 stated "No."

29. "Zozobra." Wikipedia. Wikimedia Foundation, February 12, 2021. https://en.wikipedia.org/wiki/Zozobra.

30. Luders, Eileen, Arthur W. Toga, Natasha Lepore, and Christian Gaser. "The Underlying Anatomical Correlates of Long-Term Meditation: Larger Hippocampal and Frontal Volumes of Gray Matter." *NeuroImage* 45, no. 3 (2009): 672–78. https://doi.org/10.1016/j.neuroimage.2008.12.061.

31. "This Is Your Brain on Shamanic Journey Meditation." Sara Violante, May 22, 2018. https://saraviolante.com/blog/this-is-your-brain-on-shamanic-journey-meditation/.

32. Alban, Deane, Debbie Hampton, Bruce 'Rudy' Phillips, and Zeenat Merchant Syal. "How Dehydration Contributes To Depression." The Best Brain Possible, February 27, 2020. https://thebestbrainpossible.com/how-dehydration-contributes-to-depression/.
33. "Formula for Change." Wikipedia. Wikimedia Foundation, April 11, 2020. https://en.wikipedia.org/wiki/Formula_for_change.

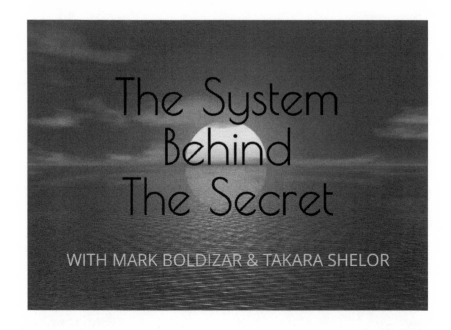

The System
Behind
The Secret

WITH MARK BOLDIZAR & TAKARA SHELOR

Prefer to learn by watching and listening? Let Mark and Takara walk you through the 5 step formula in this 6-week online course. As Jack Canfield said, "go from where you are to where you want to be."

Inside this powerful eCourse, you'll:
- Learn exactly how to get more of what you want and less of what you don't
- Discover how your thoughts create the life experiences you have
- Understand the three critical factors that determine which thoughts become your reality
- Find out what's been standing in the way of all that you desire

https://newscienceofsuccess.com/the-system-behind-the-secret-ecourse/

About Mark

Mark Boldizar is an award-winning scientist, author, visionary, personal and business improvement specialist. Mark's experience includes over 30 years as a scientist and technical leader working for multiple global corporations. Mark has worked and taught around the world, including on three continents and in ten countries. Mark has become known for delivering tangible results through the practical application of scientific principles. He has a way of teaching highly technical principles in ways that are easily understood by people at all levels.

Using his highly developed scientific approach, Mark turned his attention to understanding and experimenting with the Law of Attraction (LOA) which he prefers to call The Universal Law of Creation or simply The Law. He developed a model that explains everything that must be in place to manifest the things you desire. The model not only reveals all the components necessary to successfully program the Universe, but also what needs to be addressed if you haven't been achieving the results you desire. *Unleash Your Future* was written to be the "how to" manual for engaging The Law in a way that enables anyone to manifest the success of their dreams.

In 2019 Mark co-founded The New Science of Success with Takara Shelor, coauthor of *Unleash Your Future*. Mark's mission in life is to change the world for the better, one thought at a time. His work and the focus of the New Science of Success is to teach others how to unleash their futures by intentionally programming The Law.

Mark was Jack Canfield's guest on Episode 1 of Jack's TV show, *Talking About Success*. Mark has been seen on Roku, Amazon fire tv, Sony Crackle, Google Chromecast, and Apple TV. Mark has also shared the screen with Jack Canfield and Lisa Nichols.

Mark lives in Pennsylvania with his wife Julie and daughters Mikayla and Hope.

Find out more about Mark's work at www.newscienceofsuccess.com.

About Takara

Takara Shelor is a bestselling author, speaker, engineer, and consultant. She is known as the *Spiritual Treasure Hunter* and helps people discover the diamonds and gold within. She helps them recognize their Divine gifts and talents and find their passion, purpose, and joy. They learn how to regain confidence, heal the trauma drama of their past, attain personal freedom, and live a joy-filled life. Her mission is to help people become empowered, embody their Magnificent (Divine) Self and radiate that into their world.

Having enough of stress, she left a high-paying engineering management career in the pharmaceutical industry to move to an island and start a non-profit for dolphins and whales. She took a deep dive into personal empowerment, energy healing, and spiritual growth.

Turning her Industrial Engineering skills of continuous improvement and finding the root cause of issues toward the human condition, she developed numerous methods to help people experience more happiness and fulfillment while achieving their dreams.

She teaches how to apply real world savvy with spiritual finesse, making life easier, less stressful, and much more fun. For decades her revolutionary manifesting methods have helped countless people manifest new relationships, switch to or launch new careers, improve their finances and health. In her own life she's become a bestselling author multiple times, lived on a million dollar yacht in Fiji, owned numerous sports cars, closed a business deal in 5 minutes, and got divorced in under 2 hours (51 days is the norm in New Mexico).

She's the author of several bestselling books including *Peering Through the Veil: The Step-by-Step Guide to Meditation and Inner Peace* and *Dolphins & Whales Forever*. Takara's transformational product lines assist with physical, mental, emotional, and spiritual wellbeing. Her email newsletter, *Here's to Your Magnificence*, has thousands of readers from over 100 countries across the globe.

She provides personal, author, and business consulting, teaches numerous workshops, offers 1 on 1 consulting, and has many additional books underway.

Takara lives in the beautiful Blue Ridge Mountains of Virginia with her son, Jess.

Visit her website at www.MagnificentU.com for more information about the products, programs, and services she offers. Get two free guided meditations or a free ebook as her thank you for visiting.

Made in the USA
Middletown, DE
19 May 2021